# When You Rise Up

## Wisdom for moms who want to parent with purpose

Lee Sumner

ii

# Acknowledgements

### To My Parents
With loving memory of my dad and admiration for you, Mom: Thanks are inadequate for all the sacrifices you both made, for all the good things you taught and continue to teach your children, which have been the building blocks for a great foundation in life and in parenting my own children. I love you.

### To My Friends
*Patti, Lydia, Megan, Brenda*
Thank you, sweet friends. Thank you for the encouragement in my life's journey from the days as a young mom to the days of planning weddings and learning to be an empty nester, for encouragement to teach and to write, and even how to get published. Thank you for the countless prayers for me and our girls. Your special friendships are true gifts to my life. Thanks to the Christown Chicks who continue to spur me on. To all of you, thanks too for the beautiful examples of Christ that you each have been to me.

### To My Daughters
*Lindsay and Sarah*
I have loved being your mom. You made parenting seem easy because you are such amazing people. Thank you for loving me despite my failures. You are precious and dearly loved. Thank you for allowing me to share our lives in this book in order to encourage other moms. You are both our joy and delight.

### To My Husband
*Richard*
You are always my greatest encourager, friend at all times, partner in parenting, partner in ministry, editor of books, the anchor in our family. You are the love and laughter in my day. Your unconditional love has given me the courage to grow. You are my treasure. Thank you for making the adventure happen.

iv

# When You Rise Up

*Wisdom for moms who want to parent with purpose*

## Contents

vi

## Introduction

I am not writing this book because I have it all together as a mom. In fact, I am far from the perfect mom or the perfect wife. Not even close. I'm not nor ever have been the "soccer mom" or "super mom" type that you hear about either. You probably need only ask my husband and my children, for they are keenly aware of my weaknesses, frailties and failures. The older I get, the more I am aware of my shortcomings and neediness too.

But thank God for grace: the grace God gives freely through Jesus Christ my Lord, the grace that cleanses and covers my sin, my mistakes, my faults through His love and sacrifice; the grace others extend like my ever-patient husband and precious daughters who, though knowing I'm not perfect, seem to love me anyway; and the grace I've had to learn to give myself for not being perfect; the grace to listen, to learn and sometimes even to laugh at life and at myself. None of it has come very easily, so I am grateful for all this big and amazing grace, which has been my encouragement to press on and make progress through life despite myself.

In spite of failures and frailties, I am writing this because I love being a wife and a mother. Every season has had its own pressures and problems, but also triumphs and treasures. Being a wife and a mother has been the greatest adventure of my life.

My life was drastically changed because of my roles as a wife and mother. I'm forever grateful to God for bringing my husband and my children into my life. There have been many things that I've learned through them which have brought great joy and meaning to me. Sometimes, however, they have been the sharp instrument in God's hand used to chisel away the rough, hard edges in my life, not necessarily pleasant experiences, but needed nonetheless. What an amazing thing God does by continually using them to teach me eternal, life-changing truth. These lessons continue though my daughters are grown and married and Richard and I enter into yet another decade of marriage ourselves. Their presence in my life has also helped me to understand and enjoy the deep, deep love that God has regarding the people He created, especially those who He has intertwined in my life in one way or another. Life is a marvel, a mystery, and most certainly a miracle.

I am writing this book to hopefully encourage other wives and mothers, as you journey through life in these roles too. There is probably no greater challenge than these responsibilities, but surely nothing as sweet and sacred either. The foundation of this book is based on several Biblical truths that have been key to my development as a woman and thus in my role as wife and mother. One of them is from the New Testament in Titus 2:3-5.

Older women are instructed to encourage the younger women *to love their husbands and love their children*. It's important for women to listen to the wisdom and experience of those who have "been there and done that." The Titus 2 women in my life have put skin and bones to what the Bible instructs us to do. There were not too many of these around when I was a young mom, so I have a soft spot for younger women who need the encouragement but maybe don't always know where to get it.

It was such a blessing to me to see people living out what this should look like. I've benefited greatly from older, wiser women (and older, wiser men too.) Many of my role models taught great truth from the Bible. Others demonstrated these truths in their actions and attitudes. All served to bless me and I hope to return the blessing to those who might read what I have written. It is my desire that you'll discover encouragement from the truths from the Bible and true life stories you will find in these pages.

What does it mean to encourage? Encourage simply defined is "to put courage into someone." There have been many times I have needed the courage to do something—especially raising children. God through His Word and His Titus 2 women have given me, and continue to give me, the encouragement to do what I have needed to do in bringing up children in this tough, fast-paced, ever changing, high-tech, sometimes scary world in which we live. I believe

4

God often sent other people who served as "pitchers" of courage, pouring from their own lives into mine. It is the essence of encouragement to receive assurance that somehow things will all work out from those who have lived through it to pass it on. It has been empowering to be shown practical steps on just how to continue on, to try something new, to let go of what didn't work, to be forgiven and extend forgiveness too. Such encouragement has given me freedom to enjoy the life I've been granted. Such wise counsel has helped me to keep my sanity too!

My hope and my prayer is that this little book will serve to continue the pouring out of the same kind of encouragement to those who will read it. So, take courage and rise up! Learn truth, live it and teach it to your children.

Deuteronomy 6:6-7 *"And these words, which I am commanding you today, shall be on your heart; and you shall teach them diligently to your sons and shall talk of them when you sit in your house and when you walk by the way and when you lie down and when you rise up."*

# Chapter 1
## The Best Job Ever

Winter Balm

I had no idea what was ahead of me that almost balmy December night as Richard and I drove to the hospital near our home in the industrial suburbs of St. Louis. Our baby was not due for close to two months, according to the doctor, but something was just not right. I had known it for weeks, but the doctor kept insisting that my recent large weight gains, aches, and general uncertainties were all common symptoms for a first time mommy-to-be. What did I know?

I had been having bad back pain all evening and had stayed home in bed while Richard had played basketball with the men's team from our church. By the time he came home, my discomfort had turned to more acute pain. We tried measuring the intervals of pain to see if it made any pattern, like a contraction might, but we weren't sure. By midnight, after a call to the doctor and to my brother (who was an OBGYN in another state), it was clear that a trip to the emergency room would be the thing to do, just to make sure everything was all right. I'd never had a baby before, so I did not know if this pain was normal for this stage in my first pregnancy or if there was more to the story. Well, was that ever a major understatement! There was more to the story, indeed!

The good news was that it was a balmy night and not a snowy night. One big concern about having this baby in a Mid-west winter was how to get to the hospital if there was a big snowstorm. We lived in a little wooded area in a hollow and when it snowed our driveway somewhat resembled the men's downhill ski slope at the Olympics. One year, having been snowed in by a blizzard for a week, for an evening's entertainment we tried to drive to the top of our driveway. Our equally bored neighbors across the street gathered at their window for their own sadistic entertainment to see if we could make it. We failed, but at least it was entertainment for all that evening.

With the possible threat of this kind of weather, my husband and his friends had been thinking of creative ways to get me to the main roads if a winter storm trapped us again when the baby came due. I was hoping they were kidding when they were checking out the toboggan in the garage, but earlier discussions about calling for a tow truck to help me in and out of the car had me thinking these people were not stable and they were open to all kinds of crazy ideas. Though I didn't think I was having a baby this unseasonably warm December night, it did cross my mind that this would be a good weather night for having a baby, avoiding that sleigh ride in the snow while in labor.

After being examined at the hospital—which no one told me was going to feel like they were going to yank my child out at that very moment—I had mixed emotions about the resulting news. I was four centimeters dilated and was assured that I might be a few weeks early for this pre-mature birth, but certainly not two months early. A baby was coming and it was coming this night. Wow! How could this be? This was not how we planned this event. I had not packed a bag nor given any thought to this possibility. There was no frantic drive to the hospital. Little did I know then that many plans I would make would not be the plan God had for us.

The other conclusion from this torture–disguised as an exam–was that our baby was breech and I was going to need a c-section. Some of you reading this might be thinking, "How could all of this have happened? How could the doctors have missed this?" Many asked these questions then, but it was not as uncommon at that time for women not to be given routine ultrasounds. My doctor simply didn't see the need to do them and at this small hospital, it definitely was the exception and not the rule. Though, I must say, I didn't see too much of the doctor during my prenatal visits anyway. I just saw nurses who highlighted on my chart all my weight gains with a bright red marker. I guess the doctor didn't want to miss that. Thank you so much.

While trying to process all this news, I did feel relief, believe it or not. The first relief was purely selfish; the pain I was enduring was going to end soon. I never shared that with too many of my friends because they were all into natural child-birth which for me translated into "how much pain can I endure and still live?" Not only did I have intensifying pain at this point, but also a fever of 102 degrees. Medication was on the way and I wasn't too prideful to take it. Something definitely wasn't right and we felt this was the right course for us.

Yet, there was also another kind of relief, a winter balm. There was a definite sense of peace, a sense that somehow everything was going to be ok. I had really felt that something was different with this pregnancy, but because I was just a "first time mommy," I was patted on the knee and assured it was just first time mommy mania. But now, I knew there was something else going on and I had not been crazy after all. At least not about this.

There was this peace, a peace that could only come from God, because none of the current circumstances would lend itself to having any such sense of peace. It definitely was a supernatural peace because I certainly was not above freaking out about such things. It was all a little crazy, but I was not afraid or worried. Richard was calm too, but then he is usually calm. So I didn't panic. It all seemed to make sense and I happily went to sleep, with an excited expectation to awaken to what lay ahead. I was really going to be a mom and it was going to be this night!

Surprise, Surprise!

As the fog lifted from the anesthesia in the wee hours of the morning of that December day, I heard strange words. Really strange words! The words were distant words of someone near me—I think it was the doctor—telling me that I was the mother of twins.

What? Twins? Was I hearing right? Was I dreaming? The only thing I was really clear about in my thinking was that I was cold; I mean I was really cold. I remember mumbling this and soon I was literally engulfed in a blanket of delicious warmth. I slipped back into a happy medicated slumber, off and on for several hours. Coming to again, still fighting through the fog of anesthesia, I began to recall the word "twins." Yes, it was true—twins. I had not one, but two precious baby girls. And for sure, our lives have never, ever been the same.

I firmly believe that there is nothing more amazing that happens to women than being a wife and mother. While that statement is probably politically incorrect, I am not talking about weddings and giving birth as the ultimate life experiences for women, though they are certainly monumental experiences unto themselves. Yet, it is not just these events of marriage or childbirth that give the greatest meaning to our lives, but it is through the living out of these life experiences that we are challenged to the core of our existence. Being someone's wife and someone's mother is an amazing thing. We are shaped by these experiences and relationships and even exposed by them. We are who we really are when we are most vulnerable and in these relationships we often find ourselves very vulnerable.

My experience in women's ministry for the last twenty plus years has given me this insight regarding most women: we want to have a meaningful relationship and commitment of marriage with a man and we have an innate desire to give life and nurture life. These desires may manifest themselves differently to women in our culture today, but from my observation this desire exists nonetheless. And this is central to our own health and happiness as a woman. We are intricately connected to these relationships and experiences.

This should be no surprise to us if we are familiar with the Bible. The Bible tells us that we are *fearfully and wonderfully made* ... (Psalms 139:14) and the desires we have as women are part of God's awesome design for us. So, it is ok for us to feel this way about marriage and children. It's normal because it's how we are wired. We are literally woven or knit together with the desire for intimate relationships with our husbands and the desire to give and nurture life.

It is God's desire that we experience the fullness of His design and the abundance of the life He created us to experience (John 10:10), including the wonderful and surprisingly challenging roles of wife and mother. While I've enjoyed some great jobs outside the home which have been quite fun and fulfilling on some level, being a wife and mother is truly the best job ever.

Software for Moms?

While it has been the best job ever, it is not a job that hasn't presented itself with lots of challenges and the need to learn how to do this job well. Even though women may be genetically wired to fulfill these roles, I'm convinced too that we all need the right "software" package to make it work. Over the years all the computers I've had were designed to perform a certain way, but without applying the right software my computer didn't function as designed. Even though created to be a mom, I needed the Designer's "software" for help, but where do we go for the software for being a good wife and mother?

Because our little daughters were born prematurely, they had a few medical issues at the start of their lives. Lindsay, our first born, did pretty well and was with me at her birth hospital for a week before we were released to come home. I remember the first sense of panic bringing her home. What do we do now? Richard and I really had no clue. We even forgot to change this poor child's diaper for a couple of hours because she never even cried. *We* cried on the way home, but she hadn't figured it out yet. Oh my, we had so much to learn.

Richard and I had taken some pre-birthing classes which became obsolete information when our birth mode changed to the c-section. No one had prepared us for what comes after giving birth either. I think we practiced changing a diaper on a plastic doll that didn't cry, wiggle or discharge bodily fluids at us, so that wasn't particularly helpful when we had to perform these tasks on a real person. (I'm thankful that these days more information is given and available for young moms!)

The hospital also did not give us a "how to" book on raising this little person, let alone two at once. Yikes! Who can really prepare us for being parents anyway? While there was great joy, there was great stress too.

Were we going to be able to keep them alive? The responsibility seemed rather daunting in those early days.

And then there was Sarah, Lindsay's womb mate, as Richard affectionately termed this unexpected development. Sarah had respiratory distress at birth and was taken from us hours after delivery to another hospital in St. Louis, one better equipped for her needs with a full neo-natal intensive care unit. In the midst of all the things we could not have anticipated, God provided us with a great hospital and staff of people who knew how to manage our surprises!

A Future and a Hope

The most wonderful event in my life also came with great uncertainty. Would Sarah be ok? How sick was our precious, little real-life doll? I was on an emotional rollercoaster. Joy and delight lifted me up, but fear and doubt dropped me to new places of worry never experienced before in my life. And what about the finances for all this? We knew we shouldn't worry about money, but we were young and did not have that much. Would our insurance even cover some of the astronomical expenses we were incurring? I cried many tears of joy in my hospital room for the blessings of my little girls, but I also cried, "Lord, help!" I felt overwhelmed with this huge and terrifying job of mothering two babies at once. And I was prayerfully hopeful that they would survive their premature births for us to love and enjoy in the years ahead.

The beginning of the best job ever lay before me that December many years ago. It was just the start and God surely has had a plan for our lives. We all survived the pre-mature births and God showered us with friends, family and financial support through it all. It's so important for new moms to have that kind of support. My dear friend, Patti, and her husband Kevin became adopted aunt and uncle to our kids. Their love and friendship during those early years were also a gift from God that remains to this day.

There is a very encouraging verse from Jeremiah 29:11 and it says: *"For I know the plans that I have for you, declares the Lord, plans for welfare and not for calamity to give you a future and a hope."* This verse from the Bible has brought me great comfort and strength throughout many days of mothering. God's Word has truly been the software necessary for learning to be the mother He created me to be and that I wanted to be... and still want to be. The Bible continually has shown me God's direction for becoming the wife, daughter, sister, friend, mentor and minister to women according to His plan. It will be the source of direction and wisdom as mother-in-law to two precious sons-in-love that God has brought into our lives too. And I know it will be the source of wisdom that He will provide for us as we hopefully experience grand-parenting in the future.

## Discussion Questions

1. Share your own experience of having your first child. What surprised you most?

2. In your experience, what has been the most difficult part of being a mom? What has been the greatest joy? Who has been a source of encouragement to you?

3. Read Luke 1:26-38 and Luke 2:8-20.

   • Describe how you think Mary felt concerning her "greatest job" ever?

   • What do you learn about Mary from Luke 1:38?

   • What insight can you glean about her from Luke 2:19?

   • How does Mary's example as a mother encourage you as mother today? What hope does her life story bring?

4. What encouragement do you receive from the following verses as they apply to being a mother? Share your insights.

   Jeremiah 29:11

   Philippians 4:4-8?

5. Share one thought or Bible verse from this chapter that most encouraged you.

16

# Chapter 2
# What Does He Know?

One of the most valuable lessons that I continue to learn in life, is the importance of considering opinions and perspectives different from my own. This has never been easy for me, for whatever reasons that I won't try to analyze at this point. Most likely it's immaturity or pridefulness, but suffice it to say, this has been a life long growth process. But, I have continued to learn from the invaluable gift of listening and evaluating thoughts other than those originating with me. (Even though I doubt I've ever had an original thought in my life.) James 1:19 tells us we are to *"be quick to hear, slow to speak and slow to anger."* This is counsel that serves me well every day.

The school in which I have learned to be open to other perspectives has best been taught through the school of marriage. I enrolled in this school in 1979, marrying the love of my life, my best friend. Looking back, sometimes I just marvel at why Richard and I ever got together, but it has been the finest decision of my life, second only to the unsurpassed decision to follow Jesus Christ as my Lord and Savior when I was a teenager.

Richard and I met during college, though not the same college. In fact, we didn't live in the same place, until we were married. We met at a Christian campus ministry retreat in the Lake of the Ozarks three years earlier. We struck up a conversation at the close of one weekend, which led to a summer visit, which led to a long distance courtship, eventually marriage and then a life together, complete with kids; lots of diapers, skinned knees, broken hearts, braces, driving lessons, dating experiences, more broken hearts, college educations, as well as two weddings that occurred six weeks apart, and a only a few gray hairs. (Thank God for *Preference by L'Oreal*. I am worth it. Or so I tell myself.)

What's the Difference?

My campus minister was the person who married us and also the minister who gave us premarital counseling. During the course of our counseling sessions with Dean Ross, Richard and I learned that we had many differences. Some of these differences were natural male/female differences and some were personality, family background, and just individual interest type differences.

Richard's love of sports and my indifference to sports was often a source of conflict for us in our early years of marriage, but we had been alerted to this before we were married, so we were not completely caught unaware that this issue could stir up some trouble. Nonetheless, March Madness has been known to cause April Anger. Something we have learned to deal with. He has learned to dial back on the viewing of every ball that rolls across the screen, and I've learned to enjoy sports with him. But it has been a learning process.

There have been other differences as well. Richard was much more independent growing up; I was much more supervised. Richard has a very low key, laid back personality; I am a bit more fiery and intense. He likes pictures hung symmetrically on the walls; I think it's ok to have things hung a little more creatively. And why use a level when my eyeball is just fine? He tolerates heat and cold well; I have a five degree temperature comfort zone. I'm cold in the winter, hot in the summer. Hot flashes have added a whole new dynamic to my comfort zone issues.

Richard is extremely frugal and thrifty; he is the coupon king, deal maker, and just amazing financial leader for our family. I am less so, yet we would not classify me as a "big spender." But I would definitely be the spender between the two of us—someone needs to buy things!

Richard is a slower starter, but thorough with projects. I am ready to get going with new things, but need encouragement to finish, especially if something is not making progress as I want it to. The writing of this book has been slow off the press because it was easy to start, but rather involved to continue with life's distractions constantly vying for my attention. That's why needlepoint projects drove me insane; they required lots of time and tedious work. So, after several hours of only completing the stitching of a bird's toe nail, with the rest of the bird left to the imagination with years more work to make it a reality, I was quickly done with that project.

Other differences: Richard is very male; I am very female. Not rocket science I know, but this is actually a good thing to know and understand. According to the Bible, God made us male and female—different for a reason. Richard is very logical, a big picture thinker. I am more intuitive in my logic, but I like to dot all the i's and cross all the t's. I make lists. I like to check off things on my lists. And if I do things not on the list, I like to write it on my list and then scratch it off. He rarely makes lists, at least not on paper.

Once he asked me to make him a list of "honey do" projects, which was the beginning and end of my list making for him. He felt my list was so long that we'd be way past the rapture before he could finish page one. I learned a valuable lesson about our differences in that exercise—no more than three items at a time for "honey do" projects and not on a list. Actually, I just tell him what's on the list when he asks and it's usually just one thing at a time. This seems to be working well for us. It has probably saved a tree or two over the years, as well.

So with just these few differences, plus so many more, is it any wonder that we have had to be *intentional* in making marriage work? Now add children to this combination. With general male/female differences, plus family background differences, added to personality and interest differences, our parenting styles and plans were inevitably going to come together like two trains meeting head on down a single track. And we are human, so yes, there have been conflicts we have had to resolve in dealing with the raising of our children.

The Great Balancing Act

As I stated at the beginning of this chapter, one of the most valuable lessons of my life has been to learn to listen to and evaluate opinions and perspectives not like my own. And this has best been learned through living with my husband. There is a funny old saying and I think it captures one of the general differences between fathers and mothers in their parenting: "God gave children fathers so that they would have fun, but He gave them mothers so they could live long enough to enjoy the fun." Dads typically worry less about the stuff that moms worry about, because we tend to worry about almost everything. And if there's nothing to worry about, we'll invent something. (After all a skinned knee can lead to a staff infection which leads to gangrene which will lead to a leg amputation and possibly death.) Anyway the point of the saying is that children need balance.

Parenting is a great balancing act in so many ways. I believe that this is one of the reasons that men and women are different: everyone needs balance and the differences we have as parents bring this into consideration. But, if you are the fun one and he's the serious one, that's not uncommon either. In fact, it is very likely because opposites do tend to attract. We tend to marry someone with at least a few opposite ways of approaching life because they aren't like us and we liked that about the other when we were dating. The truth is, together, with our differences, we bring balance to each other and to our children. This too is by God's design.

However, as women, we have to learn to listen to our husbands and allow them to bring their innate male/fathering distinctives into the parenting arena. It continually amazes me the insight that Richard has about people and in particular about our children. I've not always agreed with him, and he certainly will tell you that he doesn't always agree with me, but we have learned to put all our information on the table to get the best possible, well-rounded perspective about parenting our kids, and most other things too. We don't always get there immediately, but we eventually get there. And this too is a learning process. (And yes, I know that men should listen to their wives' wise counsel too, but I'm going to let Richard write that book to men.)

Many times, he has been absolutely more in tune and correct with decisions that needed to be made on their behalf, even though I may have resisted this in the beginning. So many times I wanted to rescue our children from their struggles, but he saw the benefit of letting them work out their problems. This was hard! I wanted to fix everything for them, but he was right. They needed to learn to do age appropriate problem solving all throughout their lives. As long as failure wasn't life-threatening, immoral or illegal, such an experience could provide valuable opportunities for growth. How thankful I am for his insight for them. Don't deny your husband and your children the blessing and benefit of his presence and perspectives in their lives. It may require big picture thinking, which may be more the way he thinks than you. And it may require prayerfully letting go when you desperately want to hold on.

R.E.S.P.E.C.T...What Does It Mean to You?

I do believe that there are Biblical marriage roles that are important for us to follow for the well-being of our marriages and our parenting. This would include Ephesians 5:33 for women: *"see to it that the wife respect her husband."* Now, don't close the book. It doesn't say "wife, always agree with your man," but it does say respect him in the command verb tense, "see to it" or "make it happen", or "just do it!"

Respect your husband. What does that look like? Well, begin with listening to his ideas, his perspectives, his opinions. Proverbs 1:7b says this: *"Fools despise wisdom and instruction."* Have you been a fool, despising the wisdom your husband might have, resisting and even going against plans he wants for his kids? I am sure I have not always done this right and have been a fool myself. And I have had to learn this: you don't always have to have your way. Try it a different way. Different may not be wrong, it's just different. Learn to blend your ways with your husband's ways. It's generally a healthy move for the family.

I know there are some of you reading this who may be single moms, or maybe spiritually single, wishing that you had a godly, sensible man to help you raise your children. But a wonderful promise is given to you from God's very own heart in Psalms 68:5—*"A father to the fatherless and a judge for the widows, is*

*God in His Holy habitation."* You are not alone, and neither are your kids. It's so important for you and your children to know that God will be a husband to a woman who does not have one and a father to her children. Now, this is not in the physical sense, of course, but God is able to do *"exceeding abundantly beyond all that we ask or think, according to the power that works within us."* (Ephesians 3:20) What do you need your heavenly Husband/Father to provide for you and your children? Why not talk to Him and let Him know you desire Him in your life to help you? He is waiting for you! Watch what He'll accomplish on your behalf!

If you are married and your husband is struggling with fulfilling his God-given responsibilities as a true spiritual leader, remember this advice from 1 Peter 3: 1-2 *"In the same way, you wives be submissive to your own husbands so that even if any of them are disobedient to the word, they may be won without a word by the behavior of their wives, as they observe your chaste and respectful behavior."* The issue of submission and respect for a man is paramount to understanding how he is wired. Respect, for a man, is as great a need as is sexual intimacy. And to give him respect, even when you don't agree with him, is to demonstrate a maturity that will bring peace to your life and maybe even win your husband to Christ. Respect does not mean you can't discuss differences, it just means don't dismiss his ideas. Listen to him.

The Lord still desires a Christian wife to honor and respect her husband's leadership even if he is not a Christ-follower. God is not asking women to disobey moral laws given to us in the Bible, but most husbands, believing and non-believing husbands alike, are not asking their wives to commit murder or hold up banks. There are exceptions, of course, because men do make wrong choices just as women do, but many husbands just want their wives to let him be a man and make decisions without constant criticisms. This is the issue I am addressing. Sometimes we mean well as wives, but act as though our ideas are the only right way to do things. To allow your husband to be a man and the family leader is a life changing principle in marriage! It surely was for me. It is really a matter of remaining true and obedient to the way God has designed the family.

How's That Working for You?

Have nagging and criticizing brought good results in your marriage? Is that working for you? Does it bring you the results you desire? My survey among women who continually nag and demand control, show a big fat zero on the success scale. I've even done it myself and found that not only did my nagging and criticizing not work, but it even had adverse results in our relationship. Proverbs 12:18 gives this word picture, *"There is one who speaks rashly like the thrusts of a sword, but the tongue of the wise brings healing."*

Does your tongue slash or sooth? I confess—I was a slasher. Our culture is all about sarcasm and jabs, both for humor and making a statement. Yet, trashing each other with words is a damaging habit to fall into, especially so with our mates and family members. With God's help through the years, I've matured and know to let the moment pass in which I could get in a good sarcastic jab! While it may feel good to win a heated verbal battle, the consequences are never worth that temporary, shallow victory. We may win a battle, but a battle against our husbands is a battle against ourselves.

Consider this from Proverbs 16:21: *"The wise in heart will be called discerning and sweetness of speech increases persuasiveness."* Kindness is much more effective in persuading than harsh, angry words. This is true for dealing with our kids, and certainly true in talking with our husbands. It's true for any relationship. It's surely the way we want to be treated when others would disagree with us, right? Who wants to be cut with a knife or jabbed with sharp words? Do you like bossy, sarcastic people humiliating you with words, insisting their way is the right way? I certainly don't. I am sure Richard doesn't especially like it either. So, the question is: how can we work together more harmoniously with our husbands as we parent our children? It begins with understanding our differences and letting them bless our families rather than destroy them.

What does your husband know? He knows a great deal, but as wives, we have to be humble enough, wise enough, and willing enough to listen. Listen to your husband. Let the father of your kids be the father. Don't deny him a strong presence in your children's lives because you think you always know what's best. As far as it's humanly possible, if he's a functioning, sane person (clinically speaking), your children need the balance of both mother and father.

Allow God to bless your family by supporting your husband's unique perspective as a man, as well as his unique qualities, which most likely are very different from your own. You'll probably find that he wants your support and affirmation too, and that he actually is wiser than you may think.

## *Discussion Questions*

1. Share one or two differences between you and your husband that first attracted you to him before you were married. Has this changed? If so, why do you think it has changed?

2. Name one parenting difference that you have with your husband that may be a difficulty for you. Why do you think it is difficult? (Be sure to be respectful toward your husband if you are sharing this in a group.)

3. How does Philippians 2:3-4 encourage you to see your husband's unique perspective?

4. Is there any area in your marriage that you need to give your husband more respect? Is there something in which you know he needs your verbal support? How will you show him respect this week?

5. Reflect back on the following verses from this chapter and write out how you can apply them to your marriage today.

Proverbs 12:18

Proverbs 16:21

James 1:19-20

Ephesians 5:33b

30

## Chapter 3
## Who's in Control?

The Bottom Line

Over the years, there have been many important messages I've had to learn, but two amazing yet simple truths stand out in regard to co-parenting with my husband. First, are you ready for this?? Include him in the decision making process!! Well, there's a novel idea, but actually it is part of the Biblical bottom line for all us gals.

I can't record how often I hear women making parenting decisions, as well as other decisions, without even discussing these things with the one with whom they made a vow to "be one." We are not "one" if I'm calling the shots and he's in the dark or told to stand in the corner while I do it all the right way. How can this be a partnership? How is this oneness and honestly, how is this even helpful? The answer: it isn't.

When we ask our husband's opinion or input on anything, it is a great way to let him know we value what he has to say. But be sincere. When you genuinely want to know what he thinks, he will know it. If it's to manipulate, he probably knows that too. So when you ask him for his opinion, be ready to receive it even when it is not what you want to hear. If you regularly reject it, he will quickly learn that he has no voice with you.

Fight or Flight?

Is your husband fighting you for leadership in the home? Or is he in flight to get away from your leadership? He may try to fight you for that leadership or he may feel so defeated that he'll eventually abdicate his leadership to you. While he may not leave in the physical sense, many a husband has left the home mentally and emotionally. Some husbands will just shut down. Many men pull away from their wives and home responsibilities because their wives take charge and run the program, so he just follows a path of least resistance and gets out of the way.

Richard and I have counseled with many husbands who feel it doesn't matter what they think or try to do anyway, because his wife will wrestle him for every decision until he's down on the ground and he's tired of the fight.

Too many men retreat from being the husband and father they have been called to be because the wife won't let him be a man. She knows best and he quickly learns to stay out of her way. And if he should interject something she doesn't like, and she's quick to dismiss his leadership and counsel, many husbands begin to withdraw.

Later a wife will wonder why he doesn't help with the children and why her husband is distant from her. Rejecting his leadership robs a man of his God-given fatherhood desires, dreams, and responsibilities. Are you guilty of robbing your husband?

When Richard used to travel extensively on business, I was home with the kids and in charge of all the stuff that needed to be taken care of on the home front in his absence. Over the years I had learned from wiser ones than me that I needed to keep him involved in the family happenings and decisions, even when he was out of town on business. Daily we communicated and I would update him on the news of the day and ask his thoughts on decisions that needed to be made. This helped me feel his presence in our home and he didn't feel so disconnected when he got home. Our girls knew, too, that he was still involved in their lives on a daily and personal basis. Sometimes disciplining took place while he was away, but never without his input or knowledge. This was not because I was incapable of doing it alone, but because we are a team.

Too Much Guidance?

Even with that pattern of working as a team, it was often hard for me to let go of the reigns when he returned home. Once when I picked him up from the airport after his long week away from us, I began giving him a little too much, shall we say, "guidance" on how he was driving. He turned to me and thanked me for my help, wondering how in the world he managed to survive his business trip without it. Silence ensued for awhile and I concluded it was more difficult than I realized to share the reigns of life with him, while letting him lead as a man and as a father too. But, we are both still a work in progress this side of heaven and we managed to be able to discuss this and laugh about it too.

What Page Are You On?

The second thing I have learned that is so important for all parents to do is to get on the "same page" in their parenting. It is quite ok to have different opinions and plans, but hash these out (kindly, of course), developing your parenting strategy behind closed door sessions together. Emerge from your strategy room united and clear on what page it is that you are on. If you don't do that, your kids will see right through you and know how to play you like a well-tuned piano. They quickly know who is the "softy" on this and who is the "toughy" on that. And when the two of you are not in agreement, your kids know it!

When one or both girls approached us with a request or proposal we tried not to give our kids a decision until we had both discussed it and made sure we were on that same page. Good thing, because many times, we were not. We had to learn to make decisions together and then support each other. We were a team. This was more of a challenge for me as the mom, since I spent more time each day listening to requests. "Mom, can we have a horse?" Ok, I didn't go to Richard with that one. I *knew* we were of one mind without asking!

The Secret Ingredient

But sometimes times Richard and I could not agree on the exact plan, yet a plan needed to be made. There is a secret ingredient that really should not stay secret. It's also an ingredient that is quite misunderstood at times by women and men, but it's truly what will make your marriage and your parenting most fruitful.

When we had differing opinions on our parenting plans or direction, it was important for me to be obedient to God's word regarding the direction and attitude I needed to have at this point. I could argue and battle my husband or I could yield in deference to his leadership in our home. This doesn't mean God gives him a blank check to do whatever he pleases. A wise man listens to the counsel of a wise wife. But the Bible is clear to us gals that our husbands are to be respected as the head of the home and we are to trust that God can work through his leadership, even if it isn't perfect. And it usually isn't perfect, so that's not even the issue. 1 Corinthians 11:3 says, *"But I want you to understand that Christ is the head of every man, and the man is the head of a woman, and God is the head of Christ."* There were—and still are—simply times I yielded to his leadership and we went with his decision because we wanted to follow God's plan for resolving an issue we disagreed on. It is important to note too that his decision may at times have been my preferred course of action. When I share my thoughts in a gentle, kind, not hostile way, he usually hears me better. A wise husband will listen to the wise counsel of his wife, but a wise wife doesn't demand her own way.

True Women's Liberation

Defer to a man? Many women just absolutely shut down on this point, huffing out statements like "the Bible is anti-woman" and it teaches "women are to be doormats." This is absolutely ridiculous thinking. The Bible is very pro-women and pro-family. In fact,

Jesus Himself was very pro-women. Let me share a few examples of this.

We can begin with Jesus' connection with a Samaritan woman at a public water well, as told in John 4:7-26. Jesus engaged in a conversation with this woman, though it was very politically incorrect for a Jew to associate, not only with a Samaritan, but a woman! That culture did not regard women too highly. Women were property, much like they are today in many countries and cultures around the world. But Jesus talked with this woman because He cared about her and wanted to meet a need in her life. He was very interested in her well-being.

Other examples that support God's positive attitude toward women is brought out in Luke 8:2-3. Luke mentions three women who helped finance the ministry of Jesus and His disciples: Mary Magdalene, Joanna, and Susanna. Their contribution was important enough to find its place in Luke's gospel, recorded for all eternity.

Jesus also had two dear women friends—Mary and Martha—whom along with their brother Lazarus hosted Jesus in their home. These dear gals are mentioned several times in the Bible. They spoke freely to Jesus about their feelings and He spoke freely to them about solutions for their needs, just the way friends talk with each other. Remember, women were not considered equal to men in that day and age, so this friendship was quite revolutionary for its time. Can you imagine having Jesus over for dinner and have him come out to the kitchen to deal with your frustrated feelings? (Luke 10:38-42) Ladies, we serve an awesome, liberating, pro-woman God!

Additionally, in the Bible women are called "fellow heirs" with men and the Bible clearly instructs a man to treat his wife rightly as described in 1 Peter 3:7. Peter, an apostle of Christ, (also a married man as we learn from Matthew 8:14) wrote that men need to treat their wives in a gentle and understanding way, not lording it over them or dominating them. Right from the Bible, God commands a man to do what is right toward women. He does not want a woman to be a doormat, punching bag, or abused by a husband in any way. Jesus came to emancipate women from bondage and abuse. No other belief system in the world—then or today—values women as highly as the Lord of the Bible.

So to condemn the Bible's teaching, suggesting that women respecting men—and in particular a wife respecting and honoring her husband's leadership in the home—as anti-women rhetoric is to not have knowledge of the Bible or the God who inspired it. Modern day pro-women, anti-men rhetoric actually undermine marriages, families, and ultimately women.

If you want to look at real oppression of women, check out how they are treated around the world in other cultures and religions. I have several missionary friends who ask me to pray for the women in their countries. In many countries women are treated as property, having no rights. They are not permitted to work and have no legal rights to their own children. Those belief systems belittle and deny the value of women. Only the Christian faith sets women equal to men in all respects.

God's Equality

While the cry of some in our modern American culture is that women are oppressed, let's be real. In our country, women enjoy great freedoms! But sadly, I constantly witness the battering of a man's worth and integrity in order to exalt women. There seems to be a great deal of men bashing in our culture today. If you watch TV at all, you can't miss it. Many commercials and sit-coms show men as weak and stupid, inferior to the woman. That simply isn't true or necessary in God's economy. Men and women are equal in value to Him and in purpose, though our roles may be different. Recall, different isn't wrong, it's just different. Our culture, perhaps, needs a lesson in tolerance regarding the equality of men and women as well as education regarding Christianity's view and value of women.

Having said all this, rest assured all you moms out there, that it is quite ok, then, to have different roles as parents. As I said earlier, balance is such a vital, healthy thing for our children. Kids need a mom *and* a dad. It's best that way, even though some capable, brave men and women single parent their kids with success. However, they will be the first to tell us that this is no small challenge, difficult at best, and would attest that co-parenting is a much better ideal than going it alone.

Who is Really in Control?

When a decision needed to be made on parenting issues and Richard and I were at a stalemate, I learned the value of yielding to my husband's leadership. Was it always easy? No, but nothing of real and lasting value is easy, if you think about it. The greatest value of yielding to my husband's leadership has been that I was obedient to God. This kind of obedience continues to teach me about trusting God and living in His blessing.

There was also great value in supporting my husband and valuing him as a man. It has bred trust and partnership between us. Many times he has listened to my thoughts and counsel and heeded it too. I think this is the way it is supposed to work. Ultimately, couples must learn to trust God above independent thinking and work together to discern what the Lord has desired for our kids.  Then we seek to follow that plan together.

The wisest man who ever lived wrote this analogy about relationships and God: *A cord of three strands is not quickly torn apart.*  (Ecclesiastes 4:12b) One strand, one person is pretty weak.  Two strands may be stronger, but still weak, but a cord with three strands is not easily broken.  This is a picture of the strength we have in our marriage relationship with Jesus Christ as that central binding and unifying third cord in our marriages.

It's much easier to be on the same page or follow my husband when I remember Who is ultimately in control.   That's the key to understanding 1 Corinthians 11:3.  *Christ is the head of the home. God is the head of Christ.*  Ultimately, we answer to and are led by our Lord, the Strand that ties our marriage and family cord together.

God's truth from the Bible is our instruction manual on raising kids in order to have happy, healthy, and holy children.  And for wives to successfully parent with husbands, we need to obey God's Word in our marriages, letting Him lead us together. So, who is in control of your life?

42

## Discussion Questions

1. Share one positive quality that you respect about your husband. This can be anything. But it needs to be positive and honoring.

2. How does God's view of women, as discussed in this chapter, encourage you as you consider His command for wives to respect and follow your husband's leadership? How should this change the way you understand your role and responsibility to support your husband?

3. While we may disagree with our husbands on different issues, what do these verses say to us about the way we are to treat him whether we agree or not? Discuss your answers.

   Romans 12:9-10


   Galatians 5:25-26


   Ephesians 4:31-32

4. How can we encourage our husbands to follow his God-given leadership, but not act as his Holy Spirit or his mother, but as his helper and friend?

5. Look up each verse and consider what insights they offer to encouraging your husband in his leadership role.

   Proverbs 15:28

   Proverbs 16:21-24

   Romans 12:16-18

   1 Thessalonians 5:16-18

6. Share one thought or verse that impacted you most from this lesson.

# Chapter 4
# Parenting 101

Be the Parent

I know you have seen it. We see it all the time too. Maybe we are even guilty of letting it happen ourselves from time to time. There is the child in the grocery store throwing a hissy fit for the candy. After mom's repeated "no's" she finally gives in. Child: 1, Mom: 0.

We love our kids so much and their love and affection mean the world to us, so we give in. Sometimes we give in because our kids just wear us down. Unfortunately, we may make our parenting decisions based on the hope of providing their happiness and maybe even winning their approval or yield to their demands because it's just easier.

As a mother, there is nothing wrong with wanting our children to love us and feel that we are good parents to them. But when we try to seek their approval through decisions we make, we can become emotional hostages to them. This is really harmful to parents and children. The first thing we must learn as parents is to simply be the parent. Mom, be the mom, not the girlfriend, buddy or pal.

Start Early!

We could not believe it. One of our girls was only six months old when we realized that she was quite aware of the meaning of "yes" and "no." She had been crawling near the fireplace hearth in our family room. We didn't want the girls to be hurt from the sharp, rough surface of the hearth, so we would not allow either baby to play near it and would physically remove them. When they got close to it, we would pull them away and tell them "no."

One day, as one of them crawled away from us toward the hearth once again, Richard called out to her, "no." Instead of removing her this time, we decided to watch just to see what she would do. She had been told "no" on so many attempts to check out the forbidden fruit. (Sound familiar?) Her little head turned back to look at her dad. Then with eyes fixed on him she extended her little hand up in the air toward the hearth. Richard repeated the instruction, "no." She stopped moving forward, but she inched those experimenting little fingers even closer, continuing to watch our response. He told her "no" once more and with that, she smacked her defiant little palm against the bricks, still looking to see what we would do!

It was amazing. She deliberately disobeyed us at the ripe old age of six months and we had a choice: we could let her get away with it, deny that she made a deliberate choice, think it was cute and marvel at the intelligence of our child, or we could demonstrate a consequence for her disobedient behavior. Yes, my friends, that was disobedience. We knew we had to choose to be the parent and it wasn't easy, but it was an important moment to establish our authority as parents, even to a six month old child. Don't be surprised at how early kids challenge your authority. So be ready and establish early on what age appropriate consequences will take place for disobedience.

Parent or Pal?

Too many parents in our culture today are trying to be all things to their children. We may find ourselves caught up in this too. We want to be the "fun" mom. We want to be the perfect provider, protector, peer, and pal. We like the idea of being our kid's buddy and best friend. We sometimes find ourselves wanting our children to be the smartest and best liked kids on the block or at school. We want them to be popular and liked, because they are very popular and liked by us. Or maybe it's because we want them to have or be what was or is still missing in our own desire box.

Unfortunately, parents may find themselves making compromises in what is ultimately best for their kids in order to make their kids happy or popular. Some parents want all this so much that they lose sight of the vital parenting role and relationship with their kids. They begin to compromise parental responsibilities in order to gain an inappropriate affection. They want their child's approval above what may be best for the child. We have to ask ourselves this question: Is the goal of our parenting their happiness or their holiness? Ultimate happiness is a result of holiness, but it takes time and energy and a consistency by parents to guide them toward holiness.

Hang in There, Mom!

When our girls were teenagers, we saw altogether too many parents giving their children freedoms that were popular with their kids, but ultimately compromising in their values. Curfews were lifted too soon, "responsible" drinking privileges given, and immodest, sexy cloths were options for their highly hormoned high schoolers! They reasoned that their kids would be off to college in a few years, so what was it going to matter now anyway? We even knew of parents who allowed drinking parties to take place under their roof in order to teach their children to drink responsibly. We could not believe our ears and eyes! While these parents were certainly more popular with their teens and their peers than we were, we saw how compromises led to disasters including not only crashed cars, but crashed moral values resulting in sexual promiscuity and even teen pregnancy. Not to mention the disregard of the law.

For others, the reluctance to continue strong parental influence was simply that the parents were worn out. These parents were just too tired of fighting the demands of life—job, spouse, finances, home, future—and it just was easier for them to go with the flow of their children's wishes. It probably *is* easier and more fun to be their friend than deal with their resistance to our authority. But who said being a parent was going to be easy?

Many times I was tired of being the one who had ideals and standards and felt a little worn out myself. Fortunately, I was not alone because my husband and I partnered together in parenting. And we did get a little tired together. We didn't want to be the bad guys, but sometimes we looked like the bad guys for doing what we believed to be the right things.

There is emotional and physical energy involved in taking time to teach and correct our kids, as well as emotional and physical energy to make tough decisions. When we lighten up too soon in holding onto the reigns of raising kids, especially under the social pressures of other parents and even our own children, everyone in the family ultimately loses. Hang in there, Mom! It's a tough job, but it is not impossible.

Trying to raise you kids by winning affection and not taking action with discipline is problematic. Making such parenting decisions or indecisions may be well intentioned, but misguided and not beneficial for either parent or child. It's misguided in that it will produce quite the opposite result. Children will quickly learn how to manipulate mom and dad. Our observation has been that in these situations it is the children who are training the parents. And what obedient parents at that! Kids who know they have the upper hand with their parents don't respect them. They don't honor them during childhood and it often continues through adulthood, with increasing harmful potential.

If parents don't take their responsibility seriously, we are enabling our children to disobey. Life long disobedience is costly to kids. Children are commanded to honor their parents in Exodus 20:12. This is the only commandment with a future blessing given. If children honor their parents the blessing is that *"your days may be prolonged in the land which the Lord your God gives you."*

Practice What You Preach

If your children don't honor you, even at an early age, ask yourself some tough questions.  How have you honored your own parents?  How do you honor your in-laws?  How do you honor people who hold positions of authority in the community such as police officers or other community leaders?  Children learn by example.

If we want our kids to respect and honor us, we need to provide them the example and practice what we preach.  It's imperative to show our own parents the kind of love and respect that we want.  Do you honor your in-laws?  Someday, most likely, you will be an in-law.  What are your kids learning from you about these relationships?  How do you treat other people in general?  Do you treat them as you want to be treated?  There is a great old saying that much of what we teach our children is not actually *taught*, but *caught* through our own behavior.  What do your kids catch you doing in terms of how you treat and talk about others?

Proverbs 30:12 has this teaching for us: *"There is a kind of man (person) who curses his father, and does not bless his mother.  There is a kind who is pure in his own eyes, yet is not washed from his filthiness.  There is a kind—oh how lofty are his eyes! And his eyelids are raised in arrogance."*

Have you ever seen people who roll their eyes, lifting their eyelids in arrogance to someone? Have you ever done this to someone, maybe even your own parents? Ouch! I know I did and it makes me sad to think now how I dishonored my parents when they were trying to give me guidance for my own well-being. While most children show disrespect to their parents at some point in their childhood, are we still guilty of this as adults? As adults, do we show our parents the respect they deserve simply because they are still our parents?

Notice that we are not told we have to agree with our parents, just as we may not always agree with our husbands. Many times we will disagree. I know people who have had very difficult childhoods because their parents made horrible choices and as children they suffered terribly because of them. But even if we don't agree with our parents, we are not given permission to dishonor, disrespect, or ditch them. It is normal to disagree, but we are to show honor and respect while disagreeing. How do we do this?

Forgiveness Is Key

One of the most amazing examples of forgiveness was lived out by a dear friend of mine. Her father had sexually molested several members of her family, including her when she was a young girl. She had no memory of this until later in life when the abuse continued to the next generation and was eventually exposed. There was a horrendous upheaval in this family, resulting in the father going to prison. The mother had an illness that required her adult children's care and my friend struggled with loving, honoring, respecting and forgiving, not only her father, but also her mother for not protecting the children.

But, while she did not agree with her parents' choices, she knew that ultimately her obedience was to the Lord and not to her feelings. Have you ever thought about this? While our feelings are legitimate in that we are created to feel, we are not to make decisions solely based on how we feel. Often feelings can deceive us and cause us to justify and perpetuate hurt and anger. Haven't we all been guilty to be obedient to our feelings rather than to do what is right?

My friend was hurt and broken, but she chose to give honor and forgiveness to parents who had failed her. It's important to understand that honor and forgiveness do not mean that the other person is excused from their sin or removed from the consequences of their sin. But what my friend chose to do was this: she helped care for her sick mother, eventually wrote to her father in prison and visited him. She even told him about Christ's atoning work on the cross for his sin.

And she began to pray for her parents. And she prayed. And she cried and was angry, and she prayed. She struggled and then she prayed some more. It didn't happen overnight, but eventually there came such a healing in her that it is hard to describe in words. It was God who did the work as my friend chose to follow His commands. The Lord blessed her obedience, freeing her from the anger of abuse against her.

The final chapter was not written with just her change of heart and attitude. While in prison, her father accepted Jesus as His Lord and Savior. He experienced a true transformation that only God can give and sought forgiveness from his family. While it is still not a perfect situation, there has been a restoration and wholeness brought back to a family that was so broken. I believe my friend was used by God to accomplish this purpose. What an example she set for all of us and what an example this Godly mom has been to her children.

It Will Spill Out

As I have observed people throughout my life, I am convinced of this truth: hurt people hurt people. Do you know someone like that? And if we have been the one hurt, if we don't deal with it rightly, we'll continue to pass on the hurt too. We may need to forgive our parents (or other people too) in order to be effective in our own parenting. If we carry around bitterness from our past it is bound to spill out somewhere in our lives and most likely it spills out on those closest to us. Be assured of this: it will spill out. Hebrews 12:15 warns us that bitterness *causes trouble* and *defiles many*. To forgive and get rid of anger and bitterness is one of the most valuable gifts we give our kids and ultimately ourselves. To live out forgiveness is an incredible gift to give our children.

When our girls were in their early teens they suffered great hurt and rejection by some other girls in their so called "circle of friends." It was not just an isolated incident but an on-going way of life over a long period of time. As the story evolved and unfolded, it was disclosed that the root of the problem was with the mother of some of the other girls. And then I was hurt and angry because she had been in my "circle of friends."

It was one of the most difficult times in our lives. I knew that so much of my daughters' healing in that situation depended on my response. But my mama bear protective anger for them was a fierce animal and it wanted to be unleashed. Vindication was desired. I wanted to tell people off. I wanted apologies. However, God convicted me to do what was right. I needed to practice what I preached. So, outwardly I did the right thing. I chose to forgive.

This choice wasn't about how I felt because I felt hurt and mad. But the choice was about what I knew I needed to do. I chose to talk with the offenders and move through the hurt feelings even though I didn't get the vindication or apologies. Through that process, I learned we needed to ask forgiveness for some things too. So humbling myself, I asked for forgiveness. My girls did the same, even though the others never saw the need to seek ours.

I will be honest and tell you it took a few years for my feelings to catch up with my responses. I did the right thing outwardly, but still had hurt feelings that needed time to heal. There was not a true restoration of friendships, but it wasn't because we didn't put forth our effort to forgive and restore. A great verse that continues to encourage me to respond as God would have me to, especially when I don't feel like it, comes from Romans 12:18: *"So far as it depends on you, be at peace with all men."*

God wasn't asking me to make all things right, but *I* needed to do what was right. I needed to seek to restore the situation, seek forgiveness for my own sin in the situation and then entrust the rest to God. This has been quite a freeing spiritual discovery. I was able to move on and not allow this hurt to consume me. My girls sought forgiveness for their part in the situation too. This allowed them to move on too, not letting hurt consume them.

Then an amazing God-thing happened years later when my girls were in college. One of the girls who had participated in the "junior high junk" attended the same college as my girls. On a weekend retreat mutually attended by these three girls, this young lady sought forgiveness from one of my girls for the situation that had taken place so many years before. It was so healing! This brought a sense of closure for us, even though not all parties had done this. We were just so blessed and the Lord used that confession to tie a ribbon on a package we had wrapped up when we made the decision to forgive. It had been a choice to forgive, not based on our feelings, and now even the feelings were healed.

Another wonderful postscript to this is that as a result of this season in her life, one of my daughters now serves in ministry to young teen girls to encourage them to follow Christ, to love one another and do the right things in their lives too. God never wastes the difficulties in our lives. He allows them for our good.

It is very important for children to learn how to forgive by observing how we do it and live it. I have to confess, I have not always done this perfectly, but when I have walked in forgiveness I have seen the fruit of it bloom. Our children's ability to do what is right will be greatly enhanced by our example and the reward will be so sweet. Proverbs 10:1b says this about children whether son or daughter: *"A wise son makes a father glad, but a foolish son is a grief to his mother."* How very true.

## Making the Distinction

As we raise our children we are always to demonstrate kindness, friendliness and affection to them.   Ephesians 6:1 warns us "*don't provoke your children to anger.*"   It is a clear directive to fathers, but the principle applies to moms as well.   We are not to intentionally and manipulatively frustrate our kids.   We are not to provoke them to anger.

To be clear, however, the Bible is not teaching that if they are frustrated with our parenting, we are parenting them wrong.   Don't be misled.   There will be times when our children will get mad and frustrated at us when we stand in the way of something they want to do that isn't right for them.   We can expect it!   This is only human, right?   Remember the warning from Proverbs 22:15a that tells us "*foolishness is bound up in the heart of a child.*"   And we can't be afraid to say "no" to things that are not right.   We must be willing to give tough truth at times to our kids even when we know they are not going to like it.   We have to learn and practice the distinction between frustrating them in our own anger or manipulative desires and giving them the honest truth, helping them work out their resistance to it.

Have Big Fun!

However, being the parent doesn't mean you can't have fun. In fact, it's important to have fun!  It is great fun being a parent!  Have big fun!  Don't lose the vision for distinguishing yourself as your child's parent, but don't miss the opportunities to enjoy life with them and laugh at the lighter side of life. Laughter is great.  God made it, so exercise it. There is plenty of opportunity to guide them through everything from manners to morals, but don't miss the humor God has given us to keep it all in balance.

The M & M Moment

When our girls were about four years old, their great-grandma passed away.  They had only met her when they were six months old, so really had no relationship or memory of her.  She lived far away, but we decided to make the trip to Iowa to be with the family for the funeral.  Because of this, we had to take the children to the funeral with us.  Thus began our preparing them for the serious occasion.

A key part of this story is understanding that our girls, especially one, was known for her lively chattering and constant questions. We not only needed to prepare our two 4 year olds regarding what a funeral was all about, but we also knew we had to prepare to keep them quiet.  M & M's were our solution.

As he dressed for the funeral that morning, Richard put a bag of M & M's in his suit jacket pocket. The girls were to sit in-between us at the service and if they began to get restless or chatty, Richard had the candy handy right there in his pocket to occupy them. So off we went.

Everything was progressing normally, as funerals go. It was quiet and somber in the church sanctuary. The open casket was front and center, surrounded by beautiful flowers. All was going smoothly until out of the blue our precious, curious child shouted out, loud and clear for all to hear, *"who's in the box?"*

Just as fast as those words echoed out in the church—but clearly a minute too late—out came the M & M's, a handful shoved into one little mouth and a handful into the other little mouth just in case there was any follow-up questions or additional commentary forthcoming from the other mouth.

Sadly, no one but me and Richard seemed to have to control laughter, which made it even funnier to us. This was a great moment in our lives. Our M & M moment! Children are children and it's great for us to be able to enjoy them and their innocence and the funny things they do. Don't miss your great M & M moments either.

Being the parent means we have this role of parent for a lifetime. Of course, our relationship does change with them over time as we all mature in life, and as they become adults. We do eventually take on a more mentor/coach role. But while they are developing in character and stature, we are not just a playmate for them or the Santa Claus for all their wants and whims. It really is not our job to be their entertainment provider. But it is our job to be the parent. So be the parent. But it is highly recommended to do it in love and do it with laughter.

*"A joyful heart is good medicine, but a broken spirit dries up the bones."* Proverbs 17:22

## Discussion Questions

1. Share your observations about how parents in our culture today try to be a pal rather than the parent. What problems do you see with this approach to parenting?

2. How does forgiving your own parents (or others who have hurt you) help you as a parent? Consider the following verses as you answer this question.

Ephesians 4:26-27

Colossians 3:12-13

Hebrews 12:14-15

3. Read Ephesians 6:1-4.

- What instructions are given to children in this passage?

- Name two or three observations you make in regard to parents' responsibilities in these same four verses.

- Why do you think Paul included this teaching to the church in Ephesus? What do you think prompted this?

4.  Share some successes that you have had as a mom in having fun with your children without sacrificing your parenting principles with your children.

5.  Hopefully, you can laugh about some of the things that your children have said and done.   Share a funny parenting story that you have experienced. Why is laughter important to being a good parent?

6.  What was most helpful or encouraging to you as a mom in this chapter?  Share your insights.

# Chapter 5
# Parenting with Purpose

Get Out the Instruction Book

When in doubt about how to do something, what do people normally do? We go to the internet or some instruction manual for guidance, right? When in doubt, get out the instruction book. And then read it! It is no different when it comes to our kids. There is a great instruction book provided to us by the Creator of kids! Psalm 127:3 tells us that *"children are a gift from God."* Our very generous God has given us a priceless gift in children. And along with these gracious gifts He also has provided instructions on their care and feeding—His Word!

The Bible is our greatest child-rearing instruction book! The Lord instituted marriage and family long before He even instituted the church and has given us plenty of practical help in His Word for bringing up healthy, happy, and holy kids. God has given us instructions throughout the Bible about parental roles and responsibilities, particularly through the child rearing years. What are some of the Biblical roles and responsibilities we have as parents?

One significant conclusion my husband and I have found from the study of scripture on parenting is this: we must be purposeful in parenting.

Be Purposeful

We have been doing a bit of re-landscaping in our backyard this year. It all started with a tree that we didn't want. We also wanted a little grass and different decorative rock bordering the grass. (For those of you who don't live in the desert, desert rock yards are a norm, and grass is not a natural occurrence. However, weeds grow just fine in the desert as they do everywhere else.)

This project has been a process! First, the tree had to be chopped down and removed. This was no easy task and took quite a bit of time to accomplish. Next came preparing the ground for grass and rocks, which included first raking up the old rock, removing weeds, bricking in the area which we were going to plant sod, and installing a sprinkler system. As I'm writing this book, the project is nearing completion and has pretty much gone according to the plan. It has been a lot of hard work, especially on the part of my husband, but the finish line is in sight. It's been fun seeing the plan come together.

Being purposeful in our parenting also requires having a plan and carrying out that plan, just like the backyard make-over. Parenting is not as simplistic as a yard project, of course, but there is nothing on this planet that falls into a perfect order without a lot of work and effort. Gardens left neglected choke from weeds, and will wither and die. Cars not on a regular maintenance plan break down and are useless at best, hazardous at worst. Laundry doesn't clean itself and toilet bowls don't sparkle without cleansers, time and effort. Marriage relationships will suffer without intentional nurturing and so the same is true for our parenting. Raising kids needs to be purposeful and intentional or, as with all other things that need attention but don't get it, consequences will follow. Successful, purposeful parenting begins with a plan. What's your plan? Do you and your husband have one?

What's the Plan?

A life changing verse for me and one that was great as a plan for raising children comes from 2 Timothy 3:16-17. This is a great passage of scripture, that when applied, is a powerful, purposeful parenting plan too.

*"All scripture is inspired and profitable for teaching, reproof, correction, and training in righteousness that the man of God may be complete, equipped for every good work."*

The word *inspired* literally means "God breathed." God breathes and amazing things happen! God's words are powerful! He spoke and the universe came into existence. His very words created light in Genesis 1:3. Can you imagine? Are you picturing the significance of God's Word? We learn from John 1:14 that God's Word even became flesh. Christ, the Savior, came and lived on earth to help us understand who God is. Jesus is the very Word of God, embodying the nature and character of God. He is God in a bod!

God's Word is not just another book. The same breath that spoke the universe into existence, not only offers redemption for our souls through Christ, but gives us truth for living every day life, including truth for how to parent our kids. If we could truly accept and embrace God's Word in this light, how it should utterly change our lives! Of course, this was the Lord's thinking in giving it to us in the first place!

If we are going to be purposeful in our parenting, we need a plan. But remember to plan together with your husband. Over the next few chapters we are going to look at how to develop a parenting plan based on these two verses. Let's consider four key action words in the 2 Timothy passage.

Parenting with a purpose means putting these four action words into practice: Teach, Reprove, Correct, and Train in righteousness. The result, prayerfully, being that our children will be equipped and complete for God's purpose and work in and for their lives. How does all this work? How do we apply this in a practical way? For the remainder of this chapter and Chapters 6 through 8 the primary focus will be on what it means to teach our children. We'll examine the command to reprove, correct and train in Chapter 9.

But before I continue, I think it needs to be said that we are not suggesting that if you always do A, you'll always get B as the result. We may do all the "right" things with our children yet we may not see the "right" results. It doesn't mean that we failed as a parent. Children may choose to be disobedient and walk away from God's truth. We can't force them to know Him. God doesn't have any grandchildren, only children.

But if we know the right thing to do and fail to do it ourselves, that's our disobedience to God. I am to walk in faith as God has directed and leave the results to Him. This includes how I live as a wife, as a mom, as well as in all other relationships. The point of all this is really about being obedient myself.

## Teach

Therefore, being obedient and purposed in parenting means we need to teach our children. We need to teach them pretty much everything from manners to morals and especially teach them what it means to be righteous. Since mothers typically spend more time with their children than fathers, you have extra opportunities to instill what values you and your husband want your children to have. While we can enjoy the benefit of educational professionals supplementing our teaching, the job of teaching children God's Word and God's ways is not the job of the pastor, the church worker, the school teacher, the childcare giver, good friends or our own parents. It's our job as parents.

## A Lifetime Job

Parenting is a fulltime job and it's a lifetime job. You can't hang up your parent tool belt at the end of the day and say, "Ok, done until tomorrow." It's a 24/7/365 day of the year assignment for about 18 years under roof and then there are still parenting roles we have with our kids when they are grown. If you didn't sign up for that army—too bad, you're enlisted now! Your children need you to be a brave soldier for their well-being. But take heart, there's lots of help and hope in this parenting army!

Even When You Chop Lettuce

When our girls were about ten, we were making dinner together one evening. Our family room and kitchen were a combined great room and we had the evening news on while we were chopping the lettuce for the salad and setting the table. The headline news began with a startling announcement about the then famous basketball star Magic Johnson's AIDS diagnosis. Because my husband was and is a huge basketball fan, the big names in sports were known in our household. But what was not known in our home was the answer to "what is AIDS?" This was not something I even wanted to talk about with my kids. Why should they have to know about the bad things in life at such an early, innocent age? But there it was. And at that moment, it was me, the mom, needing to respond to my daughters regarding the ugliness in the world and the answer to "what is AIDS?"

As I considered this whole scenario for a moment, I realized I had an opportunity to teach and I wanted to do it right. I wanted to explain this with the perspective that God has on all this. After all, God loves people, but He does not love some of our actions or choices. And sometimes there are consequences for our actions. And some consequences are harder than others, having more severe ramifications. It was an uncomfortable moment in parenting, but one that needed to be met head-on in a way that ten year olds could comprehend. And it was a great opportunity to teach truth in a very natural setting. It brought to mind this passage of scripture in Deuteronomy 6:6-7: "*And these words, which I am commanding you today, shall be on your heart; and you shall teach them diligently to your sons and shall talk of them when you sit in your house and when you walk by the way and when you lie down and when you rise up.*" Or even when you are chopping lettuce and watching the news.

This passage doesn't say that teaching our children about God and God's ways are optional. Just as the Ten Commandments are not the Ten Suggestions, we are commanded to be the primary teachers of holy things to our kids. These verses are written in imperative or command language. It's what we *must* do; it's what we are expected to do according to God's plan.

And When You Rise Up

We should also draw another important conclusion from this passage: If we are going to expect our children to listen to teaching regarding God's ways and His Word, then *we* must be in right relationship with the Lord ourselves. What you teach must be evident when you walk, when you sit, and when you rise up and do whatever it is that you do every day of your life. This means our teaching is more than our words; it is who we are and how we live. We are a walking message by the way we live. Our teaching will be evident in what is on our minds, what comes out of our mouths, what we have around the house, what we drink, what we eat, what's on our TVs, bookshelves, computers, movie and entertainment list—everything. Being a purposed parent means practicing righteousness ourselves. We cannot teach what we do not know or what we do not practice. Sure, we can say it, but to say it and not do it is probably more harmful than not living it at all. Children hone in on hypocrisy like a laser-guided missile.

This is not to say that we won't make mistakes. We will make mistakes. But we must not make the mistake of walking far from God and close to destruction. We must choose to walk close enough to God that when we do fail - and we will fail at times - we are more readily convicted of the truth. And we must acknowledge to God, to ourselves, and even to our kids that parents need forgiveness too. 1 John 1:9 is such a great verse. *"If we confess our sins, He is faithful and righteous to forgive us our sins and cleanse us from all our unrighteousness."*

It is important for our children to see that we go to our heavenly Father and confess our sin. This too teaches them the right example. Is there something in your life right now for which you know you need to seek God's forgiveness? Do you need to seek your husband's forgiveness?    Maybe, you need to seek your child's forgiveness.  Remember God is right here to help.

To Love and Fear God

A few years ago, Josh McDowell wrote a wonderful book called *Love is Always Right*, speaking to the importance of teaching our children to love and fear or reverence God.  It is out of this true love and respect for a holy and righteous God that the desire to live righteously will come.  We can impose rules and regulations, but without relationship, without a heart for the Lord Jesus Christ, there may only be temporary obedience to us and to Him.  Rules without relationship may ultimately lead to rebellion.  All we have to do is look at history to see that this is true. Forced religion and rules have never changed hearts, unless it was to harden them against God.

Relationship is always what God is seeking with His children.   When we have a relationship with our heavenly Father, we understand that certain rules are meant for our good.    Boundaries are for our protection.  We trust the Lord because we have a relationship with Him.  When we have a relationship with someone who loves us and whom we love, we tend to respond to them in obedience more readily. We trust them.

The most important thing we can do for our kids is to introduce them, hopefully at a young age, to the person of Jesus Christ.  As the parent, you have the greatest opportunity to share with them about a saving relationship with the Lord.  As a mom, this should be our focus in shaping their character and conduct!  And it begins with living out our own personal connection with a loving God and our obedience to Him.

In the first two chapters of 1 Samuel we read about a father, who was also a priest in the Jewish Temple. His name was Eli.  Eli was serving God, taking care of the things of God, and was even used by God to give a barren woman, Hannah, great hope and good news. God was going to answer her prayers for a child and Eli was God's messenger for this great news. However, we learn some sad news about Eli's own sons in 1 Samuel 2:12. The Bible records that Eli's sons were *worthless men; they did not know the Lord.*

Here was a man who loved and served the Lord, but who raised children who were worthless and didn't even know the Lord.  What a grief this must have been for Eli.  While the Lord held the sons ultimately accountable for their hard hearts and evil choices, we learn of the mistake that Eli made—he disobeyed God with respect to his children's sin.  The Lord held him accountable for his responsibility as a parent.

There is no guilt trip intended here. Sometimes children do grow up and reject their parents' wise and Godly teaching, so this is not to say that all parents of wayward kids are like Eli. But, clearly from God's own words, Eli was disobedient to God. Our kids will ultimately answer for their own choices, but we are accountable for our choices too (See Chapter 10 for a more detailed explanation on Eli's parenting mistakes.)

It should be encouraging to us that the Bible shows us examples of parents who failed to help us avoid some similar mistakes. We can't force our children to accept Christ as their Savior; this is a work that only God can do. It is our responsibility, though, to teach them about God in all that we say and do, so that they will see Him modeled in our lives and hopefully desire a relationship with Him too.

## Discussion Questions

1. Share how you came to know Christ as your Lord and Savior. (If you have not made that confession, turn to Page 167 for a brief explanation of what it means to accept Christ's invitation to become a child of God and how you can respond to this invitation today.)

2. Discuss one thing that you are currently trying to teach your child or children. What are some of the

greatest challenges you have experienced in this process?

3. What encouragement can we glean from these verses as we experience the challenges of practicing the truth in our own lives and then teaching our children truth?

   Galatians 6:7-9

   Ephesians 6:12-13

4. Read Deuteronomy 6:4-9. How important did the Israelites consider it to teach their children about God? Describe to what extent they did this. Then share ideas about how you can apply these same principles to the teaching of your children today.

5. Share one verse or thought that most encouraged you from this chapter.

# Chapter 6
# The Battle for Morality

Welcome to the Battle

We live in a day and age where moral impurity is thrust continually in our faces. It's on and in magazines, books, movies, TV, computers, restaurants, billboards, clothing stores, and anywhere else you can display a message or hear one. Commercials flagrantly tease with themes of adultery, fornication, homosexuality, lewdness, and sensuality of all types. Food advertisements even sell sex as they try to sell us a hamburger. How can we teach and protect our kids from the onslaught of impurity and immorality? It's a battle we must engage and, by the Power and Spirit of God, see the victory! So, my friends, welcome to the battle.

Recognize the Enemy

There is a definite war going on for the hearts and minds of our children. Truly, there is an enemy against marriage and families. I believe that the enemy of our children's souls wants to corrupt their moral conscience as early as possible. It is vital for us to recognize this enemy and do battle for our children's moral purity. If the enemy can sear their conscience early in life, it is easier for him to deceive their heart and mind for the rest of their life. If they have seen, heard, and experienced sexual promiscuity from toddler to teen years through the convenience of our modern day technology, they can be virtually desensitized to discern right from wrong unless there is some intentional training to battle the cultural war for their hearts and minds. There will be nothing that isn't the norm and therefore "no big deal" when it comes to moral contamination. The enemy has infiltrated and indoctrinated our culture by disguising his agenda in cartoons, movies, books, TV, internet, education process, as well as government and social policy. There's really little disguise left.

Under Attack

The attack often begins on a personal level with the preoccupation with self-image. All of us are vulnerable when it comes to the social will for "fitting in." None of us like being left out or sticking out in our circle of peers and this is especially hard for kids.

And it's critical for us as parents to help our kids establish their self-worth as a child of God at an early age, so that their esteem anchor is in Christ, not in their culture.

It's important to teach our children how to act and even dress with moral purity goals in mind. As a parent of girls, I found this to be rather challenging. Even when we desired to do the right thing, the clothing choices were often limited. As the mom, I truly didn't want my girls to feel like social outcasts, but I knew I couldn't allow them to follow the course of society without restraint. So we had to develop some boundaries that would help us to choose clothes that were somewhat trendy, but not trashy. So, I developed a little mental test for this, which I later dubbed as the "3B Test." Though my girls are grown, I still use this rule for myself.

The 3B Test is simply this: Before going out of the house evaluate these three things in connection with the clothing choice you've made: *Breasts, Belly Buttons and Bottoms—if they show, you're not ready to go!"* If your daughter's dress or top reveal her breasts or cleavage, put another layer under it. The layered look is still in! Or buy a top that covers. The layered top also helps with jeans or pants that ride lower that the belly button. But with pants, there are degrees of lowness, as you probably know from your own shopping and certainly from observing the trendy garments of our times.

Just today, Richard and I were out having lunch when a young woman came into the small restaurant. She was a pretty girl, but wore a very skimpy top with sweat pants worn so far below her belly button that a little stretch the wrong direction could have brought a breeze in the valley, if you catch my drift! My eyes caught his when she came into his view and shaking his head with a sad chuckle, he headed for the men's room until she had purchased her lunch and left. (How I valued my husband's sensitivity!) The girl's clothing was bad. Yet, I couldn't help but to feel sorry for her. She looked so trashy and the message she sent was that she did not value herself or have any regard about her moral purity. I don't know if she believed those things, but the message her clothing advertised was not that of a pure and wholesome mindset.

It's important to really help our children with these choices. Mom, don't buy or allow your pre-teens and teens to buy pants that are so low that a longer top can't cover up their abdomen area. Please guard against buying sexy clothes for your young children. It just sets the stage for wearing them when they are older, also exposing them to sexuality too early in life.

With young guys, we see that they have no issue of wearing their pants so low that we get a view of their little hind ends too. If not their hinies, we get the view of whatever underwear they don't mind sharing with us.

What is up with all this? Why are parents allowing their kids to be trashy? Why are parents pushing their children to be sexy? Are we not living in the most sexually promiscuous time in all of history? Is it any wonder our kids struggle with this?

Check Your Own Mirror

Mom, how are you dressing? Are you the right role model for you kids? As women, we should learn to dress to draw attention to our face and our eyes too, not our body curves, so we need to check our own mirrors as well. Help your daughters to dress in such a way that people, especially guys, will desire to meet her eyes and see her beautiful countenance and observe her Godly character, not her beautiful body that she needs to save for her future husband. Mom, are you demonstrating this by the way you dress too? Remember, more is taught by what is caught in our actions and attitudes, including the way we dress.

How do you want your sons to view women? What kind of girl do you want your sons to be attracted to? Men and boys are sexually aroused by sight and we need, as Godly wise women, to dress so that we don't cause men—young or old—to struggle with sexual temptations. We may think we have the right to dress as we please, but we make boys and men vulnerable to temptations when we disregard their need for purity too. We must help our young girls understand this as well. This is a kindness and a love that we can give to men. It is just simply thinking about others rather than ourselves.

What's Really Going On?

So what is really going on? Let's ask ourselves a few questions. What is my heart motive when I dress? What is really going on in our hearts? Are we dressing to draw attention from men/boys? Are we dressing to impress other women? Women are brutal on other women in this area. Women berate one another for the way another woman dresses. And if it isn't stated out loud, it is surely observable in behavior. I've been with women who look me up and down, inside and out, evaluating me from hair-do to toe polish, but not engaging my eyes and my heart in honest, caring conversation. What's that all about?

As a Godly woman teaching our children, what is our own motive in the way we dress? While it is ok to dress attractively, it's important that our clothes are not to attract attention to the wrong things. Neither should we dress so freakishly out of style, seeking to make a statement about our own holiness. This sort of dress is a "me" issue too. As an ambassador for Jesus Christ, I represent *Him*, not me. Our daily clothing should reflect who we belong to. The clothing choice we make is a great opportunity for us as moms to set the standard and example.

Several years ago my then 15-year-old nephew was giving advice to my then 14-year-old niece—his cousin—who was about to start high school. Sarcastically, he told her if she wanted to make friends quickly, especially with the guys, she should wear low cut pants with a shirt that would expose her belly button and her chest. While made in sarcasm, he made an astute observation about his own culture.

As parents, let's don't give up and give in to our culture and cheat our children from living with the highest moral standards, even down to the way they dress. Teach them about moral and sexual purity, beginning with the way they dress. It involves taking time, looking at options and teaching them how to choose the best options. So begin when they are still very young. It should not come as a shock when they are teens that we want them to dress differently from what they've grown accustomed to as they grew up. You'll save yourself and them a lot of stress if purity is the goal in their wardrobe choices from day one.

Be Encouraged

Be encouraged as you keep diligent to the task! Don't let your kids talk you into things that will help them compromise themselves and others. It's amazing what kids show up in at school, church, and elsewhere that parents have personally purchased or at the very least funded. It's ok to say *no* to your child; it's ok if they don't like it. Remember, you are the parent, so be the parent! There are plenty of stylish and trendy clothes choices that don't compromise purity standards, but it requires effort and commitment not to give in to the pressures our kids can put on us. Don't let them take you as that emotional hostage to please them. When they reach the teen years, you are not finished parenting, so don't quit there. Keep going! From Galatians 6:9 we are encouraged with this basic truth about hanging in there and doing what is right. *"And let us not lose heart in doing good, for in due time we shall reap if we do not grow weary."* Don't grow weary, Mom!

The Art of Waiting

It's also extremely important to teach your children about sexual purity and waiting for sex until married. This is God's plan for our children too. So many kids are cheated out of staying pure simply because their parents did not challenge them to do so or train them in the art of waiting. Teaching our kids to wait for sex in marriage can begin with just teaching them to wait, in general. If we are constantly gratifying their every want when they want it and how they want it, they won't learn to wait.

One of the popular methods for baby feeding when my girls were born was to feed them "on demand." The philosophy was whenever they wanted to eat, that was when they were to be fed. Feeding twins (that could be a whole book in itself) was challenge enough, but that feeding on demand thing was, to be honest, not beneficial for any of us.

My babies would only take in small amounts of milk at a time before falling asleep. But then, because this was so little food for sustaining them for very long, they slept only short intervals and within the hour they wanted more to eat. And so the cycle continued. They would never eat enough at one time and wanted food often. Too often.

Imagine our life trying to feed two babies who wanted to eat pretty much all the time, never really getting satisfied, but always wanting more. Let me assure you, no one was happy with this plan. If this method worked for you and your family did well with this, I would not question you. But, this just didn't work for us on a number of levels. Here's why.

As I look back there was actually a greater principle at work in our lives. What we found was that we had to teach them to wait. I know that may sound harsh to make babies wait for food, but ultimately they were happier after we made a little course adjustment in their feeding schedule. (Now, we never let them starve, so just relax.) But, without a schedule they were constantly hungry and crying for more until there was a plan. We gradually went to a three hour feeding schedule. It was a little hard the first few times during the transition, but they very quickly learned to eat more at regular feeding times. This kept them satisfied, less fussy, and contented longer between feedings. They were actually learning to wait at a very early age.

As they grew, the intervals grew longer between feedings because they ate enough to satisfy their little tummies. They napped a little longer and were generally happier. We basically continued this plan through their childhood. We practiced waiting for meal times to eat, though there were exceptions for healthy snacks between long stretches and growth spurts when they were just really hungry. (And honestly, occasionally we did have unhealthy snacks too. We are human and enjoy junk food like anyone else, but really tired to make our habit about waiting and eating healthier foods.)

Teaching kids to wait for birthday gifts or Christmas gifts is another way to just simply train them in the art of waiting. I've seen parents just let their kids have things in advance because their kids just didn't want to wait or they didn't want to wait in giving the gift. Also, help your children wait by teaching them to earn treats or other things they want by working for them as they are growing up. Let responsibility provide reward. This helps them to appreciate the value of what they want and teaches them about the waiting process too.

The Gift of Sex

As children are learning to wait for other pleasures and treasures in life, it will make better sense to them to wait until marriage to enjoy the gift of sex. Are you teaching your children that sex is a gift? And that it is a gift to be saved for their wedding night? They are hearing different messages everywhere else. It will still be a challenge for them to wait, but if it makes sense to wait and waiting is a life style habit, they will be much better equipped to withstand the pressure and will hopefully choose to wait for marriage to enjoy intimacy. Often in the Bible we are admonished to "wait on the Lord." We too quickly rush ahead of God seeking our own pleasures and desires, only to find that we've missed God's best.

Begin talking to your children about sexual purity at young ages in appropriate ways. Encourage them that waiting will bring the greatest joy in marriage and is a gift God desires for them and their future mate to save for opening on their wedding night. Focus on the Family and FamilyLife Ministries have written many great resources for families for these topics. Check out their websites for more information and scores of books and other resources on this topic.

Vision with Value

When our girls turned 16 we gave them their own "Promise Ring"—a pretty ring for them to wear as a symbol of their commitment and promise to wait for sex until marriage. This was a deliberate challenge or goal we presented to them and one that they accepted for themselves. We celebrated with their friends and many of them told their parents and likewise received Promise Rings for their birthdays too. Of course, just challenging our kids to commit to sexual purity is no guarantee that they will, but in today's culture not challenging them is almost a guarantee that they will compromise. Proverbs 29:18 warns us with this: *Where there is no vision, the people are unrestrained.* Some translations use the word *perish* for *unrestrained.* Unrestrained means loose, wild, abandoned, or out of control.

Without a vision or direction, our lives go out of control and yes, we perish. We know this is true as we look around the world today. Unrestrained, out of control, wild living has been costly to our children and the generations to come. Give your kids a vision of God's highest best. Be diligent to teach them truth, even in midst of the ever deepening pit of moral decline. Be the parent that God has called you to be and battle the cultural tide which desires to steal moral purity. With God's help and power, this too is possible.

## Discussion Questions

1.  Share some ways in which parents can effectively offer protection for moral purity with children, especially in the early, formative years.

2.  How are children (and adults) under attack in our culture today when it comes to our self image? What can we do to protect our families from this attack?

3.  How do these verses encourage you to keep standing firm in teaching moral purity to your children?

    Psalm 1:1-3

    Psalm 138:7-8

    Romans 12:1-2

Colossians 3:1-4

4.  We are all too programmed to try to get whatever
    we want when we want it.  Why wait?  Look up the
    following verses and discuss what they reveal
    about God's perspective on waiting.   Share your
    insights.

    Psalm 25:3

    Psalm 27:14

    Psalm 37:7,34

    Psalm 40:1-4

5.  What are some practical ways that you can help
    your children to anchor their self-esteem in Christ
    and not the culture?  Seek out an older Godly mom
    and ask how she did this with her children.

6. From this chapter, share what verse or thought was most helpful or encouraging to you in regard to the battle for moral purity with your children. How will you apply this to your life this week?

# Chapter 7
# Back to the Basics

Just Be Nice

How incredible that God's word gives us guidance on almost every subject we can think of, if not directly, then certainly by principle! While the Bible does not say "Thou shall not smoke a cigarette," it does tell us in 1 Corinthians 6:19-20 that our body is a temple of the Holy Spirit and we are to take care of it and regard it as such. So, by principle, any substance abuse certainly hurts the temple of God and therefore is not a practice that honors God. And while there were no abortion clinics in Bible times, per se, we know by principle that abortion is the murder of innocent human life. (And, in case it isn't clear, to kill people who run abortion clinics is also murder.)

Then there are times when Scripture is clear and direct and we are not left to extract the principle.

Just be nice. How much more basic can it be than to just be nice? The very first Bible verse our children memorized in their initial pre-school class from Ephesians 4:32 is *"Be ye kind, one to another...(KJV)"* The Bible tells us that parents should be teaching children how to be kind, honest, and live as people of integrity. And if we're going to teach it, we'd better be doing it ourselves. If we demonstrate these principles in our own lives, the character of Christ is written in our actions and attitudes. Our life example is a more believable book read daily by our children than any lecture we could give them on the subject. If we are unkind to others, our kids will more readily learn those habits from us. If we are not completely honest and cut corners, they will learn to do the same. Kindness, honesty, and integrity begin in our hearts and are practiced in our homes.

It Starts in the Home

Mothers, when your kids see your kindness and respect towards your husband, they'll more easily learn to be kind and respectful at home and elsewhere too. Ephesians 5:33b says, *"See to it that the wife respect her husband."* It's easy to respect those who seem to deserve it, but it's the supernatural work of Christ in us when we love and respect those who may not seem to deserve it. One of the greatest gifts we can give our children is to demonstrate respect to our husbands—whether by your standards he seems worthy or not. YOU do what is right regardless of what others are doing. Isn't that what we want our children to learn? It starts in the home and with us!

The Measure of Character

The truth is being kind to others is not about their worthiness to receive it, but it is about doing what is right. It's easy to be kind and courteous to those who are kind and courteous back, but the true measure of our character is reflected when we respond rightly to everyone even when we have been wronged.

Jesus is our role model for this. 2 Peter 2:23 shows us that even when He was hanging on the cross, Jesus did not revile or utter threats against those who had done Him wrong. But, Jesus kept "entrusting" Himself to God. What a great truth to teach our children. When you are wronged, don't do wrong back. Teach them to trust God for the solutions to their relationship troubles. Teach them to respect adults, even if they don't agree with them. Our kids will learn from us how to do this, so we have to learn how to do this better ourselves.

When I was in high school, my own dad taught me this very principle on respect. When I had teachers that I just didn't like and whom I felt didn't like me, my dad would not let me just change classes and teachers willy-nilly to avoid dealing with difficult people and situations. I had to learn to respect authority, even if I didn't like that authority. I had to learn to sit under the authority of some obnoxious people in my schooling years (at least obnoxious to a teenaged girl) and learn to speak to them with kindness and respect, even when I felt they didn't deserve it. But what a great and valuable lesson I learned and have been able to pass on to my own children. While it may be true that there are mean-spirited people in the world, we don't have to be one of them! And neither do our kids.

When we show kindness and respect to others, our own children learn how to become the person and eventually the mate they need to be. It can even have an impact on the mate they choose, who hopefully will demonstrate kindness and respect to them as well. Parents are role models, so model well.

Circles of Influence

1 Corinthians 15:33 gives this warning for all of us: *"Bad company corrupts good morals."* There were times during the girls' younger years, as well as high school years, that we had to remove some friendships from their inner circle of friends. There were kids who had corrupting influences on our children, and so we had to create boundaries for different kinds of relationships. The girls were not strong enough at that time to recognize it on their own—most children are not. So, we had to help them put relationships in

different categories. There are people we allow to be closer to our inner circle of influence and those who are not allowed in those places, but whom we are kind and cordial to and befriend in a Christ-like manner. But not everyone we know needs to be in our closest circle of friends.

Jesus demonstrated this very idea of having different circles of friendships in the way He connected with others too. Not that Jesus needed to worry about corrupting influences on His perfect heart, but that He demonstrated a pattern for us to follow. Jesus ministered to the multitudes and smaller crowds of people, but they were not His closest associates. He sent 70 out two by two who worked in ministry with Him, but they were not those closest to Him, though they were certainly closer and part of His ministry. He also had a small group of 12 disciples that were much closer to Him, but only three of those—Peter, James, and John—enjoyed the closest fellowship of human relationships with Jesus. And the One whom Jesus was most intimate with was the Father alone. Parents, it is good for all of us to have these boundaries in our relationships and teach them to our children. We have different circles of friendships, but not all are equal. Or at least they should not be.

Often, our kids can't see the bigger picture on many fronts—including relationships. But it is our job to help them identify these things. It's ok to say "no" to some friendships for your kids as they are growing so that they will learn to be discerning when the choices are completely their own. This is purposed parenting.

However, say "no" with a "yes" in mind. When you have to say no, when possible, provide alternate avenues for fun and friends as you steer them in the right direction. Don't always be the "no" mom without looking for alternatives. When we had to say no to certain parties or events, we'd offer the option of having another outing or party at our house. It wasn't always convenient, but we didn't want doing the right thing always associated with unpleasantness. We didn't want good values to always be a bummer. Look for alternatives to your "no's" and allow your home to be open to your kids and their friends, with your vision and values guiding.

Mates and Models

The dating years seemed to be a time other parents we knew checked out of the parenting business. We were never sure what the thinking was behind that decision. For us, it was a time when we had to be most on our toes. And again we turned to the instruction manual for this too. The Bible provides great counsel for us as parents to give our children regarding the choosing of friendships and future mates in their lives. Take some time to look at these Bible verses for wisdom on how to instruct your children to choose mates. (Proverbs 13:20-22; 14:14-18; 15:17-22; 18:22; 19:1-2; 19:14; and

31:10-31) For some additional ways to teach your children in fun ways, read the next chapter entitled *The Necessary Nine*.

While we can give this verbal wisdom, and we should, there is still no substitute for living it out for our children to see. Mom, model for your son the kind of wife the Bible says he should seek. Do you want your son's future wife to treat him the way you treat your husband? Help him to desire to find a wife who honors her husband and who is kind and wise. As he watches your behavior, he sits in the classroom of life. Mom, model for your daughter the kind of wife the Bible says you are to be and she is to become. She too sits in your classroom on this subject. Help her to see how to value her husband and be the kind of wife and mother that will honor God.

Princes and Frogs

When your kids are dating, don't be afraid to be active in their lives. It is not only ok for you to be asking questions, it is your responsibility. Be the parent. It was a rule in our home that we had to meet the boys our daughters dated and our desire was that the boys ask my husband for permission to date his daughters. Our girls actually liked this idea and helped in making this possible. This was not always comfortable for any of us, but it was a great practice. If you have sons, teach them to seek permission from a girl's parents before dating her.

Teach him to be a prince, a son of the King of Kings. We tried to teach our girls that God sees them as His princesses and a true prince will see them as a treasure and value them enough to ask permission to "seek the treasure." And so it went.

Young men who won't go through this process expose something about themselves. Perhaps there will be a frog or two that come through the door before the true prince arrives, but it's a great process for the entire family. Teach your children that they are children of the Most High and they need to date and marry royalty too!

## Discussion Questions

1. Share what person(s) that you most admire or respect. Why do you respect him or her? What qualities do you see in their lives that you'd most like to have in yours?

2. Read Psalm 15. List the character qualities that you find from these verses describing the individual who is close to God? Name one of these that is a strength in your life? Which one is a weakness that you'd like to strengthen?

3. 1 Corinthians 15:33 reminds us not to be deceived and that *"bad company corrupts good morals."* How can we avoid corruption from wrong friendships, but still demonstrate kindness? Is it ever ok to disallow your children from certain relationships?

4. From the following verses, how do you think God feels about corrupting influences in our lives and that of our children?

   Proverbs 4:14-15

   2 Timothy 2:19-23

5. What thought or verse from this chapter was most helpful to you? What will you do differently this week in your parenting as a result?

# Chapter 8
# The Necessary Nine

One year we decided to teach our children about evaluating friendships from a Biblical perspective in a more creative way. So I wrote them a little booklet, sprinkled with fun clip art illustrations that shared our thoughts with words and pictures instead of the usual parent lecture. Sadly, there were plenty of "soap box" lectures, and while some of them may have had their place, I'm not sure those were necessarily the most effective way to teach them. When they were older, the girls would tease me that I was "sudzing" again when I got to preaching from my soap boxes! Yet we wanted them to evaluate friendships based on Biblical standards. How could we express to them in a tangible, but less preachy way that there are various categories of relationships that we have in our lives?

106

Discerning Different Circles of Friends

Like Jesus' various circles of relationships, we wanted to help our kids in tangible ways think about how to choose and place friends in appropriate categories. But how should we choose and place them in the proper place in our lives?

While we didn't want to be too legalistic about relationships, either with guy friends or girl friends, our hope was to just have a way of helping our girls evaluate and think through relationships and their place of influence in their lives. Thus was born the booklet, *The Necessary Nine*. It was to help them think about friendships in light of the nine fruits of the Holy Spirit named in Galatians 5:22-26.

The remainder of this chapter is the highlight version of their booklets. The clip art could not be included for copyright reasons. We wrote more personal things directly to our girls in their own booklets, but hopefully the basics that follow will encourage you to consider creative ways to talk to or write to your children about friendships/relationships and help you to be intentional in your parenting too!

## The Necessary Nine
(Excerpts from the original booklet)

Dear Daughter....

2 Corinthians 6:14-15 tells us that *"we are not to be bound together with unbelievers; for what partnership have righteousness and lawlessness, or what fellowship has light with darkness? Or what harmony has Christ with Belial, or what has a believer in common with an unbeliever? Or what agreement has the temple of God with idols. For we are the temple of the living God."* This charge to Christians to not be bound together with unbelievers is relevant to any close alliance. It is not to say that we are not to have friendships with those who don't believe as we do, but that our closest alliances and confidants need to meet the Lord's standards for the best in our lives. Below, with Biblical references, are some standards we want to encourage you to consider for developing any deep level of friendships and understand it is what we must expect of one another (when we marry) as husband and wife.

We are calling this the "necessary nine" because it is based on the nine fruits of the Spirit found in Galatians 5:22. We would like to put these fruit to the test in relationships that you have by asking some questions for you to prayerfully ponder.

Galatians 5:22 *"But the fruit of the spirit is love, joy, peace, patience, kindness, goodness, faithfulness, gentleness, and self-control..."*

## Love

Love is such a misused word in our language. I love dogs, I love coffee, and yes, I love you too. Gee thanks. But love from someone who has influence in our lives should cause us to ask what that love really means. What does that love really accomplish?

1 Corinthians 13: 4-8 says this about what love is and is not and what it accomplishes: *"Love is patient, love is kind, and is not jealous; love does not brag and is not arrogant, love does not act unbecomingly; it does not seek its own, it's not easily provoked, does not take into account a wrong suffered. Love does not rejoice in unrighteousness, but rejoices with the truth; love bears all things, believes all things, hopes all things, endures all things. Love never fails."*

How do your closest friendships demonstrate love toward you? Do you see evidence of the 1 Corinthians 13 love in their attitudes and actions toward you? Toward their peers? Toward their parents or others in authority in a manner consistent with the Bible? Remember, love is not a feeling, which gratifies selfish wants, but love acts with the other person's best interests in mind.

If someone tells you that they "love you"—ask yourself if this is consistent with the Bible's definition of love or with the world's misuse of the word love. If a young man says that he loves you, yet wants you to compromise sexually or in any other way...you can know for sure that he does not love you. Not the way the Bible says he should love you and not the way you would want to be loved. This is lust, not love. Don't be deceived. Remember that real love always acts with the other person's best in mind.

## Joy

As you allow people to get close to you, it is inevitable that you bring your influence into their lives, just as they, naturally will bring theirs into your life. It's just a fact of life. In a world that is often bitter and sarcastic, mean and self-serving—how very important for those close friendships that surround you be those who would shine the Joy of Christ in your life for encouragement and strength.

A joyful spirit is an indication of spending time with the Lord. Especially look at any young man in your life—if he is spending time with God's Word and in prayer, he will certainly exhibit this characteristic. Psalm 16:11 says *"You will make known to me the path of life; In Your presence is fullness of joy. In Your right hand are pleasures forever."*

Does this person generally have a joyful spirit?  Or are they only joyful or happy if the circumstances are good?  Can they have joy when things are not going well?  This is a measure of real joy—joyful when things are tough.  If they generally have a gloomy or excessively moody spirit as a way of life, this should bring you concern.

## Peace

Is your friend a person who is generally a peacemaker or a peace breaker?  Does this person have a respect toward parental authority—both publicly and privately?  Or is there constant discord between parents or teachers or any other authorities in their life?

Sometimes we do have conflict and difficulties with others and this, of course, is very normal, but the fruit of peace in our lives demonstrates the desire to resolve conflicts as far as it depends on us, as Romans 12:18 reminds us.

If you have a young man come into your life who is constantly not at peace with those who are in authority over him, this is a red flag warning.  This is an indication of a rebellious spirit.  And how does he encourage you to resolve conflicts in your life?  If this person is never at peace with himself or with his decisions, there should be pause for you to ask yourself ...why?

Consider this question: If this person is continually not at peace with God, with those in authority over his life, or with himself—would this be the kind of person with whom I would want to share a life? Would my future home be peaceful and joyful with such a one as this?

## Patience

The word patience comes from the Greek word "*makrothumia.*" Makro means "long in time" and thumia comes from a word meaning temperature of fever or passion. Some have translated patience to mean "having a long fuse." This is a good picture of patience, isn't it? Someone who has patience won't blow up quickly or ignite to passion and anger very fast. In Titus 1:7 patience is given as an important qualification for a Godly man and leader in the church: *"he must be above reproach as God's steward, not self-willed, not quick tempered..."*

So as we apply this to close relationships and those you would consider as a future mate—look at the fruit of patience in their lives. When wronged, would this person be known for being patient or "long fused?" Or would they be known for being angry and reactionary? Would they ignite quickly or respond calmly?

In a day where we see so much domestic violence and abuse of women by angry out of control men, this character quality in a future mate is so very important for you (as a woman) to discern early in a relationship. If a man is out of control with anger before he is married, he certainly will not change just because he is married.

Now he can change, because the Lord can do redemptive work in anyone's life, but the work of redemption is God's work; it's not the work of a girlfriend or a wife.

## Goodness and Kindness

Goodness and kindness are also a good measure of a person's real character. As you consider anyone to be a close friend, one in whom you would put your confidence or share your heart, would this person characteristically be good and kind to you and to other people? What have you observed? Is this person consistently thoughtful and sensitive toward others?

Hebrews 10:24 points out that we need to *"consider how to stimulate one another to love and good deeds."* How well do those who are influencing your life demonstrate goodness and kindness in their lives? Specifically, does this person influence you to be a better, caring, more thoughtful person? To love the Lord more? To obey your parents? To be honest and giving? To do good to others? Then ask yourself this: Is your own walk with Christ stronger because of the time spent with this person?

## Faithfulness

Faithfulness is another very important quality in any relationship, but especially as you consider a future mate. The Greek word used in this context comes from the word "*pistis*", meaning to demonstrate a firm conviction producing a full acknowledgement of God. This is a person surrendered to the Lord and whose conduct is inspired by that surrender. How vital for you to discern a man's faithfulness to the Lord, which will translate to his faithfulness in a marriage and to his family.

How do the friendships you are considering—those that would intertwine with your life and time—adhere to this fruit of the spirit? Is this person faithful to the worship of our Lord and Savior Jesus Christ in regular church attendance and Bible study? Is there evidence of God's character in their lives as a result of this? Do they encourage you to be faithful to worship and spend time with the Lord in His word and prayer?

How faithful is this friend to the ordinary tasks of life? School work, jobs, keeping promises, etc? How faithful is he/she at managing money?

Proverbs 12:22 says, *"Lying lips are an abomination to the Lord, but those who deal faithfully are His delight."*

## Gentleness

Gentleness has also been translated meekness. Gentleness or meekness often confuses many to think it means weakness. But certainly Jesus is gentle and meek, but there is nothing weak about our Lord and Savior. In fact, gentleness is often defined as "keeping power under control." The spirit of gentleness acts fairly, moderately, expressing consideration for others. It is a wonderful quality to have in a trusted friend. When a man can keep anger and passion under control in a loving, wise manner, he is one who imitates Jesus.

How do your closest friends demonstrate gentleness? Is that person generally gentle in words and actions? Or does this person have rough, maybe even coarse, foul, or rude language or behavior? Ask yourself—do the guy friends in my life speak to me with gentle, Godly words? Do they treat me in a manner that would represent the way the Lord wants a young lady to be treated or does he treat me like one of the guys?

As with all of the fruit of the Holy Spirit, gentleness is a quality the Lord is looking for in Godly men and women as leaders of His church and in marriages and families. Titus 3:2 concludes that those with a Godly character will *"malign no one, be uncontentious and gentle, showing every consideration for all men."*

## Self-Control

What does it mean to be self-controlled? As we look in our culture today, we see a lot of people who are controlled by themselves, doing whatever the self wants to do. But certainly this is not what the Bible is teaching. Rather, self-controlled is really yielding our self to the control of the Holy Spirit, to produce in us all the characteristics that we have been talking about.

Ask yourself this about your closest friends or possible future mate: Do they generally demonstrate self-control in decisions they make for their lives and the ones that involve you? What are their views on drinking and other forms of drug use? What about smoking?

How do they practice Holy Spirit control in what they watch on TV, movies, internet, and even the music they listen to? What has been their connection with pornography? What books do they read? What entertainment do they allow in their lives?

How do they exhibit self-control over frustration? How do they express self-control in the area of sexual purity? What safe guards have they laid down in their lives to help accomplish these goals? The answers to these questions will give you insight into whom or what is in control of a person's life. Is it the Spirit of God or some other spirit?

Daughter, as you look toward the future and meet young men, observe these things we have written to you. This observation takes time. Time is important.

Don't be in a hurry to have a relationship with a guy. Never be in a hurry to marry. Wait for the best as it is worth the wait!

Psalm 25:3 promises us this: *"Indeed, none of those who wait for You will be ashamed."*

### Discussion Questions

1. What characteristics do you think are most important in close friendships? Share some that are non-negotiables for you.


2. As you think about each of the nine fruits of the Spirit, write out how you see these growing in your own marriage relationship? How do these manifest themselves in your friendships?

3. Are there any areas of weakness that you know that you should confess as sin and forsake and allow God to work on this in your own life? Write them here.

4. Discuss other creative ways that you can teach your children about the fruit of the Spirit. If they are young you may want to choose different ways than if they are older or teenagers.

5. Share any insights or scripture that spoke to you in this chapter. How can you use this to become a more intentional parent this week?

# Chapter 9
## The Discipline of Discipline

We spent the last few chapters discussing the significance of *teaching* our children as a directive from 2 Timothy 3:16-17. We looked at some important Biblical values that parents do need to teach their kids. That's the first step in being a purposeful parent. We have to teach them what to do, what not to do, what is right, what is wrong. They don't come pre-programmed to know this stuff. After we do this, in a perfect world, they would say, "you got it, Mom and Dad. Glad to obey." But since we don't live there yet, what do we do when they have been taught what we expect and then they have the audacity to disobey?

Consistency is Key

There are a variety of thoughts on the subject of how to discipline your children. Some people are adamant that you should never spank your children, while others will contend that it's the only way to discipline them. But what does the Bible teach us?

With the Bible as our guide, we concluded that a combination of methods were appropriate, depending on the age of our children, the nature of the "crime" needing discipline, and a few other considerations. But the most important thought that we concluded regarding disciplining our children was being consistent. Consistency is key and is truly the discipline *we* needed in learning to discipline our children.

Another important facet of discipline is to be a student of your child and understand what motivates (or de-motivates) them to accomplish the ultimate goal–conforming to the image of Christ. What is very effective with one child can be absolutely worthless with another. Go the extra mile and do your homework to understand what makes each child tick and discipline accordingly.

The Bible does address some specific teachings regarding the plan to purposefully raise children. Remember 2 Timothy 3:16 which gave us our overall parenting plan? We are to teach, reprove, and correct in order to train our children in righteousness. We are not only to teach, but to give reproof and also correct. This is the training. We teach, reprove, correct. Then we do it again. Then we do it again.

It takes consistency. But what does this mean? What does it look like in reality? Let's take a look at what these words mean and how we might be able to apply their truth to being intentional parents.

Reprove comes from the Greek, meaning *to expose the truth*. It means pointing out behavior and attitudes that violate God's ways in their lives, which includes disobeying you as a parent. Reproof means telling them "This is wrong. What you did is not right. You have disobeyed me and you have disobeyed the Lord." But remember, before reproof comes teaching. Consider these passages of scripture as we think about the term reproof.

Proverbs 10:17 says, *"He is on the path of life who heeds instruction* (teaching)*, but he who forsakes reproof* (pointing out error from the teaching) *goes astray."*

Proverbs 15:31 reveals, *"He whose ear listens to the life-giving reproof* (pointing out error from the teaching) *will dwell among the wise. He who neglects discipline despises himself, but he who listens to reproof* (the pointing out of error from the teaching) *acquires understanding. The fear of the Lord is the instruction for wisdom, and before honor comes humility."*

In the previous chapters much time was devoted to what to teach our children for a reason. Before we point out error to our children (reproof), we must teach and instruct and be sure they understand the expectations. Then if they stray from it, then we must point out the error. This is reproof. Sadly, many parents don't spend enough time teaching, get very frustrated and angry when their kids disobey, and are too quick to point out error. There is much work involved in teaching. It's a lifestyle for a lifetime.

Yet, we are instructed to reprove. And we are to give the reproof, that is, *tell the truth in love*. (Ephesians 4:15) The point of the reproof is to bring them back in line with the teachings, which is about bringing them into righteousness. Righteousness is about the heart. We can probably make our kids obey, but what we really want and what God really wants is heart obedience. He wants righteousness.

Reproof should *never* be about having our way or lording our authority over them. Reproof should not be a way to vent our anger, even when they have made us angry. We can use our physical size and emotional intimidation to manipulate our children to submission, but we will either reduce them to emotional rubble or we may instill in them a rage that we never anticipated. And when it blows, it will blow big.

Reproof is about lovingly exposing the child's error, which may lead to correction or chastening from the wrong. Teaching is about "what to do;" Reproof is "bringing to light error" and Correction or Chastening means to "punish or have a consequence for."   In the Bible the term correction is often used in connection with the use of the *rod of correction*—which can be a physical punishment.

Read what the Bible says about this:

Proverbs 29:17, *"Correct* (bring a consequence for) *your son, and he will give you comfort; He will also delight your soul."*

Proverbs 23:13-14, *"Do not hold back discipline or chastening* (bring a consequence for) *from the child, although you beat him with a rod, he will not die. You shall beat him with the rod and deliver his soul from sheol (hell)."*

Now don't freak out.  This sounds so severe until you really study what this passage is saying in the original language. I was amazed when I first studied the original meanings for these words.  The words used for rod are descriptive of a twig branched off of a tree limb.   Interestingly, I recalled that when I was growing up, a little twig from a tree branch was called a "switch" and it was used as a tool of discipline!  It was a flexible twig off a tree, not a log or solid tree branch.

It's unfortunate that the word "beat" is used here because of the modern day interpretation of this word. The Hebrew term to beat is the word *nakah*—to strike either lightly or severely. And to distinguish whether the word is used as lightly or severely depends on the context around the word. So many people misunderstand the Bible because they take words out of context and misapply meaning to it. Because the word beat/strike is used with the twig implement as given in this verse, the context would imply that it is referring to a lighter strike, not a severe strike, as we tend to use the word "beat" in our language today.

So, it would not fit the context and the understanding of the words that you can severely beat someone with a light flexible instrument. The text further implies this by saying if you use the twig/switch for correction, your child won't die. To do it the way that the Bible seems to be describing won't kill your child. However, the lighter striking with a twig would and should cause discomfort or pain of some sort or what is the point?

So, as I understand this, the teaching is that a swat with a flexible tool was a method of delivering correction (consequences) for disobedience. While there should be a sting, pain, discomfort, the correction with a literal rod **should not injure or bring bodily harm to our kids.** Other verses on using the rod that you can look up include these: Proverbs 12:1; 10:13; 14:3.

Proverbs 22:15 tells us "*Foolishness is bound up in the heart of a child, but the rod of discipline will remove it far from him.*"

The purpose of the rod is to cause enough discomfort to associate that pain with sin. Sometimes the switch didn't really cause hurt bottoms as much as it caused hurt feelings. My girls knew they had disobeyed, that they had sinned and didn't like the idea of punishment. They felt badly that they were going to suffer a consequence. This is probably most effective when children are young because most cannot reason or understand with baby reasoning that their behavior is sinful. But what they can understand more easily is the association of the wrong behavior with the discomfort of a consequence. And they will learn to reason this: *I don't like what happens when I disobey mommy and daddy. I don't want to disobey. I won't do that again.*

Romans 6:23 reminds us of this important truth: "*The wages of sin is death...*" Wages are what we earn for what we do, right? Ultimately, what we earn as a result of our sin is spiritual death. But, as we see all the time, sin can lead to physical death. Sin can bring a physical death if a child disobeys his mother by ignoring the teaching/warning not to go into the street and is hit by a car. The sin of drugs and alcohol abuse kill thousands every year, even though there is much teaching and warning about the consequences. But for all of us, the payment for our sinful soul condition is death, spiritual separation from God. To chasten our children is to begin to teach them about their own sinful soul condition and their need for Christ's payment for that sin. We must learn to take sin seriously in our own lives and in our children's as well.

It is important to make sure that correction or consequences brings about true repentance. What is repentance? Repentance is conviction that my offense is wrong and I desire to change my behavior. Consequences help our kids understand the need for repentance and his or her behavior went against what they have been taught. This is easier to do when the child is older and verbal communication is developed. But what about when children are very young?

Recall that we knew that our daughters understood "no" when they were six months old, and could disobey that simple instruction. Without a consequence, teaching and reproof are incomplete. Consequences for our disobedience are not always a literal strike with a switch, but certainly some form of the "rod of correction" is necessary for several reasons. Without consequences we don't learn to change our behavior. Without consequences we would just keep doing wrong. We see the reality of this every day. It's why we have laws with consequences. It is all because we have this sinful human nature. So age appropriate consequences are actually necessary for all of us. It is part of the training in righteousness.

Four Important Biblical Principles for Discipline.

While it is important to allow and enforce consequences for disobedience in our children, it is important for us as parents to have guidelines for the disciplinary process. Here are four that we tried to live by.

1. Do not discipline in anger.

Jeremiah 10:24 *"Correct me, O Lord, but with justice; not with Your anger, lest you bring me to nothing."* The prophet Jeremiah recognized that God's righteous anger could bring him to nothing. If God unleashed His fury on all the sin that we commit against Him, there would probably not even be any ashes left as evidence of our existence. We would be nothing.

While God would be justified to punish our sin, He is merciful and sent His own Son to take the punishment for us. In a similar way, we must exercise Holy Spirit control and not discipline our children in anger and bring them to nothing either literally with physical abuse or emotionally with verbal abuse. Both are terrible and not what the Bible teaches. Correction is to bring our children back to righteousness. It is not to be so physically or emotionally severe that it would forever alienate them from us or the wonderful God who loves them, or heaven forbid, to crush them either physically or emotionally. Correction is truly all about love. It is why God corrects us and allows us to suffer consequences for our sin too, just as Hebrews 12:6 tells us: *"for whom God loves He disciplines and scourges (*or spanks*) every son who He receives."*

When the girls were about two years old they could be everywhere fast. I was young and thin then and for the most part could keep up with them, but I had to be on my toes! As a young family we were working hard to provide things for our household like all young families do. And like most families we didn't have a lot. But at that time Richard had recently purchased for me a beautiful velour chair for our living room. It was a treasure.

One afternoon when the phone rang—and I tell you the truth—I was only on the phone a minute. I knew not to be on the phone longer without a visual on the girls. So quickly getting off and promising my friend I'd call back later, I turned the corner to the living room where "Lindsay da Vinci" and her partner "Sarah Picasso" were gleefully designing their art masterpiece in hot pink magic markers, not only the wall behind the chair, but also my new blue velour chair!

I was so mad. I mean really mad. So mad that my body trembled and my little tots, clearly aware of this, quickly scampered up the stairs to their bedroom at the end of the hall. I could not even speak. I just could not believe the sight I was beholding! But I knew that I could not discipline the girls at that moment. I was way too angry. I could not trust myself to do it properly, so I just let them hide in their rooms while I cooled off.

I pondered as I sat on the floor next to my ruined chair about the whole deal. Perhaps the chair was too important too me. Surely I would need to put a lock on the drawer that had markers in it. How long had they been planning this wild artistic frenzied moment, hoping for just such a distraction on my part? We would have a long conversation about this later, but their stray from the teaching not to draw on furniture and walls was going to have to be covered in mercy. It was how I was going to be able to practice self-control. My anger could bring them to nothing. I knew it. I wanted my children to obey, but I didn't want to hurt them. Especially over something stupid like a chair.

Don't hurt your children. Please, please, don't hurt your children. Remember the purpose of discipline is to bring them to righteousness. It's ultimately what God is trying to do in my life and yours, as well as our children. Let's not forget the goal. Don't discipline in anger.

2. Discipline for disobedience or rebellion, not accidents or childishness.

It is important for you and your husband to know your children and to be objective about them. This is why two heads, two parents, are best. This was something that we knew we needed to discern together. We didn't want to be parents who made excuses for their children's misbehavior, but we wanted to be fair. Our children will know the difference between right and wrong through our teaching, but may choose to disobey anyway. This is rebellion. We have to be honest and see that children do sin, and that they sin at young ages!

We get confused sometimes thinking rebellion means temper tantrums, but rebellion can also be passive rebellion which is so much more subtle. Kids are so very smart at early ages (as we saw with our six month old choosing to test her will over ours at the fireplace). We have to be honest with ourselves in that sometimes our precious, innocent little darlings just flat out chose to disobey. And we must reprove and correct them.

Yet they will be ever so sorry if we reprove them (pointing out error) and promise so earnestly with tears and wailing not to do it again in order to avoid correction (consequences). There are exceptions, as I shared previously with my children's magic marker madness. I needed to bring *my* anger under control, and not react in it, but then not to use that as an excuse for not bringing my children to account for their misdeeds.  Our kids need us to be consistent with consequences, not forever lenient.  If you have an anger issue, this should be a warning sign to you to get that right with God quickly so that you can deal with your children's sin properly.  Remember, walk in righteousness yourself and be the parent.

But sometimes children stumble accidentally. Sometimes they do things because they are children. Their intent was not to disobey, but they have not matured enough to understand.  This is where is it so important for us as parents to understand and know our children.  If Max knocks the milk off the table because he is just a little guy and was clumsy, that is an accident.  It isn't necessary to give a consequence for that, although it would be good to teach him how to be more careful and perhaps where to place the cup more safely for next time.  But don't humiliate Max for this problem.  Now if he deliberately knocks it off because he is angry, now that is a different issue! See the difference?  We have to deal with attitudes as much as we do actions.  Such an action would merit a consequence.

Proverbs 29:15 speaks this truth, "*The rod and reproof give wisdom, but a child who gets his own way brings shame to his mother.*"

3. Discipline consistently.

Proverbs 13:24 says, "*She who spares her rod hates her son, but she who loves him disciplines him diligently.*"

I want us to focus on the word *diligently*. To be diligent means to be attentive, careful, hard-working, thorough, and conscientious. The opposite is to be lazy. It is so important to be consistent and persistent in the teaching, reproving and correcting of our children for this is what it means to *train them in righteousness.* This is the training part of the 2 Timothy 3:16-17 passage.

To be lazy is to be inconsistent. If we change the rules on our kids, they are confused with how they should behave. We are only training them that they count on us to be flaky. If one day they get screamed at and spanked for disobedience and the next day the same offense is overlooked, they don't know what to expect regarding their sin, but will quickly learn that you don't mean what you say because your responses change.

The discipline of our own disciplining is the critical issue. Generally, our children need to know that if they do X, the result will be Y. They should be able to take that to the bank! As they grow, they will learn to know you and the discipline plan for their own behavior. Parenting with purpose means first clearly setting forth rules, values, boundaries, and expectations or teachings. If children disobey what has clearly been taught then we need to reprove (point out error) and follow through with the appropriate correction (the clearly communicated consequence for that action.) When we do this, it actually takes the guess work out of disciplining. Just follow the plan.

4. Discipline privately.

Ephesians 6:4 reminds parents not to provoke children to anger, but bring them up in the *discipline and instruction of the Lord*. It is important to be careful when reproving and correcting our children that we do it in a way that will best lead them in righteousness. We are not trying to win any contest other than the one for their souls. It's not about power, but it is about love.

Also, we don't want to intentionally frustrate or embarrass our children in public or even in front of their other siblings. Publicly correcting our children may bring misunderstanding from strangers with differing opinions about discipline. Correction needs to be a private, parent-to-child encounter with a clear time of restoration. This isn't to say that others won't know about the consequences, but that as the parent we are respectful of our children as people who need one-to-one time with us to help them understand the offense and any ensuing punishment for the offense.

Our children need to know that generally they have to suffer a consequence for disobedience and rebellion, yet they must be able to see we truly do love them and that's why we will insist they go through the process of consequences.

Following whatever correction is appropriate, there must be a time of restoring your children after the correction time. If you have never restored your children after a disciplining, it is never too late to tell them that you love them and that reproof and correction in their life are not because you are mad or because they are bad or evil. Assure them that the consequence for a disobedient action or attitude is to help them to obey God as well as mommy and daddy.

As they grow, keep talking about these things with age appropriate discussions regarding the consequences of our sin and how Jesus died for our sin, so that we would not have to endure eternal punishment. Disciplining is the perfect time to share with your children the love of Christ and His plan to restore a rebellious people to a Holy God.

## Discussion Questions

1.  Share the most challenging part of disciplining your children? What specific Biblical lessons from this chapter could help you to parent more effectively?

2.  What are some key values and teachings that you have been teaching or want to become intentional about teaching your children? Are you consistent in partnering with your husband on these values and goals?

3. Review the four Biblical principles for discipling children in this chapter. Discuss which of the four was most beneficial or helpful and why.

4. Sometimes the hardest part of parenting (or doing anything) is waiting to see the results of our efforts. How do these verses give you encouragement?

Galatians 6:9

Ephesians 6:10-12

Psalm 34:15

5. Is your child or children struggling with obeying you? Why do you think this is true? Prayerfully ask the Lord if there are issues of inconsistency in your way of disciplining. Or if you have disciplined in anger, will you confess that anger to God now. Perhaps you need to seek your child's forgiveness as well.

6. Share one verse or insight from this chapter that gave you encouragement and hope as a mom. Why did you choose that verse?

# Chapter 10
# Things We Need to Know

I love that in the Bible we are given truth about the reality of our humanity. It is a truth meant to help us. We don't just see God's people being perfect all the time, but we see how people who loved God made mistakes. Now, we are not to enjoy their mistakes or follow their fallen examples, but we can learn from their mistakes without having to make them ourselves. Many of these people loved God, but they got derailed from time to time. God doesn't want us to derail, but I know He left these stories in the Bible not to condemn those who have failed, but to spur us on to the hope that we don't have to fail. We not only have the power of the Holy Spirit living in us as believers, but we have the power of Spirit-directed examples to warn us to heed the teachings and leadings of the Spirit of God. The Lord knew we would need to see this and so I am grateful for Him providing these things we need to know.

And what things do we need to know?  There are so many things.  In this chapter, I just want to share about three common parenting mistakes.  If we allow these truths to teach us, we can avoid making the same mistakes.  We have the Holy Spirit and we have His Word to show us what happened to these families who chose to parent in their own way apart from the leading of God's plan for them.  So let's visit three families and learn to avoid their parenting mishaps.

Common Parenting Mistakes to Avoid

1.  Honoring Our Children above God

As we noted in Chapter 4, the Lord held Eli, the priest accountable for his failing as a parent.  Recall that Eli had two sons who did not know the Lord and who did evil.  God surely held them accountable for their sinful hearts and misdeeds.  We read that.  But what was Eli's failing?  What did he do wrong?  After all, these were adult children and aren't our kids on their own at that point, accountable for their own choices and behavior? Absolutely true!  But, in 1 Samuel 2:29 the Lord is clear and direct with Eli about his responsibility as the parent. He tells him *"you honor your sons above Me."*  Yikes! There it is!  Apparently, God detected something in Eli's heart that needed to be exposed.  Eli gave greater honor to his sons than to the Lord.  Something was going on in Eli's heart that God had been addressing for some time.

Truly, God is dealing with our heart issues too. If Eli, a man of God, struggled with keeping God first place in his life, are we foolish enough to think we won't have the same inclinations? We need to heed the warning about not honoring our children above God too. While we are to love and nurture and cherish our children, we are not to worship our children. We are not to allow them to take the place of God in our lives.

Our kids mean everything to us, don't they? As a mother, there is not much that I would not typically do for my kids. There is such a mama bear spirit of love and protection in us that we know we would die protecting them! Right? It would not even be a second thought for most of us. This isn't a bad thing; in fact, it is how God wired us to a certain extent. The problem comes when we allow what we think is love for our children to replace our love for and obedience to God. Number one of the Ten Commandments is that we have no other gods than the Lord God Himself. As much as we love our children to death, we must not allow them to become our idols. Have you ever thought about that? Are your children idols in your heart? How do you know?

I think Eli's story will help us to understand. His feelings for his sons kept him from obeying God. If we do not teach, reprove, correct and train our children in righteousness, who do we honor more— God or our children? This seemed to be the message

142

God had for Eli.  His sons were adults and they were punished for their evil deeds, but Eli had a heart problem too.  He honored his children above God.  The best love we can give to our children is our first love for God.  Apparently, Eli came up short in this area.

Many people tell me how much my daughters look like me, but I will tell you that they have many of their father's genes.  One gene they got from him was their natural abilities for sports.  I consider walking around the block my Olympic accomplishment. But my daughters played high school sports and were very good at them.  Thus sports were a part of our family life routine.

But also part of our family life routine was to honor the Sabbath and keep it holy.  This was one of the non-negotiables for us as a family.  Sunday was the day we went to church.  So, as much as sports and practices were important, we did not allow them to become an idol in our lives.  Sadly, though, Sunday was a day that many youth sporting events and practices took center stage in many families' lives.  There were not Saturday evening services offered at these times, so many Christian families took themselves and their kids out of church to participate in sports.  Not that we should be legalistic about this, but children's sports became the family focus and habit instead of worshiping the Lord and honoring the Sabbath.  How will our kids learn the discipline of attending worship regularly, if we allow their interests and activities to constantly replace it? What are we teaching them? How is this like Eli's problem? It is honoring our children above the Lord, and certainly one area where we need to be sensitive to God's Word and not the world's way.

It's so easy to be caught up in doing all, being all, giving all to our children because we love them so dearly. Yet there is an out-of-order trap that parents can fall into if we don't honor God above all else. If we love the Lord with all our heart, mind, soul, and strength, He is going to give us the best course for loving and giving what is best to our children. Proverbs 3:5-6 is a great reminder of this: *"Trust in the Lord with all your heart, and do not lean on your own understanding. In all your ways acknowledge Him, and He will make your paths straight."*

2. Honoring Our Children above Our Husband

Our children are not to be given honor above our husbands either. Even the desire for children has caused some women to set aside their relationship with their husband and his God-given authority as protector and leader of the family. Titus 2:4 teaches us to love our husbands (*philandros*) and to love our children (*philoteknos*). These are two distinct Greek words on how to love the dearest people in our lives, but they are distinct.

Wives are to love their husbands as sweethearts and lovers and love their children with a maternal, nurturing, teaching love. One is not more important than the other, but it's important to understand and obey even how we love them.

Too many women honor their children above their husbands, forsaking the effort to continue being his lover and sweetheart, his support and helpmate, often putting children ahead of marriage. Regrettably, some women prefer their children over their husband by disregarding this relationship and his headship in the home. Then when the children leave the nest, they look at the man across the kitchen table and wonder 'who is that stranger?' It is a statistical fact that the highest divorce rates occur during the first seven years of marriage, but the second highest divorce rate occurs when children leave the nest. It can unfortunately be connected with couples who focus on their children at the expense of one another.

What Was She Thinking?

Remember the story of Abraham and Sarah? A childless older couple who could not have children, but desperately wanted them? Graciously, God promised them children and descendants that would be as numerous as the stars they gazed at every evening after dinner. But in Genesis 16 we read how Sarah became impatient with God's timing, not trusting God to fulfill His promise to her husband and herself regarding children.  Sarah became so child-focused that she impatiently ran ahead of God, His promise to her husband and took matters into her own hands.

Here was Sarah's brilliant idea: Sarah encouraged her husband to take her maid and have a baby with her. I can't even imagine what she was thinking!  Was this ever the original surrogate mom idea gone oh, so wrong or what?  So Abraham sleeps with the maid— because they didn't have invitro back then—and then things got worse.  Hagar, the maid, despised Sarah, smug and arrogant with the fact that she conceived a child with Sarah's husband.  Can you just feel the fire between these two women?  Sarah hated Hagar and Ishmael, the son Abraham had with Hagar.  Then Sarah blamed Abraham for the entire deal.  What a mess! And, by the way, what was Abraham thinking?

First, lest we totally barbecue Abraham for apparently not objecting to this whole arrangement, consider the culture in which they lived.  This was not an unacceptable worldly practice for barren women to consider for giving children to their husbands.  It was shameful for a woman to be barren, so this was a culturally acceptable practice. Women did whatever worked to be able to give their husbands a child. With this background, we have a little more insight into why Sarah pushed her plan forward.  It's not an

146

excuse for running ahead of God, but it was her reasoning. Yet it was not God's plan.

It's easy to criticize Sarah's solution to their struggles, but let us ask ourselves this question: how many of us compromise God's ways because "everyone else is doing it?" Men and women have sex and children outside of God's plan for the family all time, then look to the culture for ways to justify it. But surely, the Bible is clear that God's ways are not our ways! (Isaiah 55:8-9). Sarah did not wait for God's timing to bring about the answer to her heart's desire.

And while we can surely point fingers at Abraham like his wife did, I have often thought about this: Abraham did not think of this idea himself, but unfortunately followed the counsel of his wife. She must have felt so desperate and he must have loved her so much. Have you ever thought about that? Abraham was willing to try this crazy thing, compromising his trust in God to appease the desperation of the woman he loved. I wonder how many times we have been guilty of urging our husbands to do something in which God has not given him a peace or a blessing to go ahead!

We could spend an entire chapter just on the importance of not influencing our husbands to disobey God, but we'll suffice it to say that Sarah led Abraham to action rather than waiting on what God has promised. This caused great grief not only to that generation, but to all the generations that have followed. Sarah dishonored her husband's leadership, not trusting God, and ran ahead of God with her own ideas. Abraham had not been worried about God's plans for their future and their children. But Sarah didn't respect her husband and pushed him for another solution. As a result of her disrespecting her husband, we daily witness the on-going struggle between Israel (descendants of Isaac, Abraham and Sarah's son of promise) and the Arab nations (descendants of Ishmael, son of Abraham and Hagar.)

What a great lesson for us as wives and moms as we consider the eternal significance in honoring and respecting our husbands as we discussed earlier. How we treat one another and how we follow God's plans will be reflected in the legacy we leave behind.

I remember vividly talking to my husband about having children about two years into our marriage. I was ready to have a baby and he was reluctant. It wasn't that he didn't want children, but the timing was not right in his mind. He felt that financially we were not prepared for this. I didn't like his plan, but I allowed him to show it to me on paper. He carefully laid out our income and current expenses to allow me to see why he was concerned about having children at that time. We had a property to sell first and then we could move forward with family plans. So, reluctantly, I agreed with his plan to wait.

Within a very short period of time we were financially free to move forward and voila—you know the story—we had twins!  God sees the future that we cannot see and desires us to trust Him for that right timing in our lives too.  He gave my husband that caution and wisdom to wait, knowing what He wanted to accomplish in our lives.  And because we waited we were able to afford, without serious financial worries and burdens, the blessings of our two daughters.  Whatever parenting decisions you are making, don't rush ahead of God's plan as He leads your family through the headship of your husband.  Don't become so child-focused that you lose sight of God's plan for your family.

3.  Favoring One Child Over Another

The story of Isaac and Rebekah is such a wonderful love story gone wrong too.  Isaac was the promised son that God gave to Abraham and Sarah, the one through whom He intended to bring about the nation of Israel. After Sarah's death, God brought a wonderful gal into Isaac's life, Rebekah.  Isaac and Rebekah started out great! Rebekah, having some difficulty conceiving too, finally gave birth to twins—Esau and Jacob.  Having twins, I know what a blessing this must have been for the happy couple. But sadly things quickly went sour.

We read right away in Genesis 25:28 of an all too common parenting mistake.    *"Isaac loved Esau because he had a taste for game, but Rebekah loved Jacob."* These parents had favorite children. Isaac loved Esau because he was a man's man. Esau loved the outdoors and hunting like his father. But Jacob, apparently, was more like his mom. Surprisingly, Isaac and Rebekah did not seem to even try to hide their partiality! Rebekah's favoritism for her son Jacob caused her to deceive her husband in a conniving way and pitted her sons against one another. She certainly honored her son above her husband and her other children.

Most seriously of all, she interfered with God's plan. God intended for Jacob to receive a blessing and, as promised by God for only reasons that God decided, Jacob was to receive the first-born blessing rather than his twin who actually arrived first. Rebekah definitely wanted Jacob to receive this promise, but God's promise apparently was too slow in coming to suit Rebekah too. Rebekah saw an opportunity to get honor for her son, Jacob, but at the expense of her other son, Esau. Not to mention the expense of her relationship with her husband. She didn't wait on God's way, but ran ahead with her own plan. Sound familiar? You would think she would have heard about her own mother-in-law's errors! What a mess we make of our lives and our children's lives when we play favorites. And what a mess we make when we take action apart from God's leading.

Rebekah lost her family in the whole tragedy. Jacob was sent away to protect his life from his outraged brother. Esau married ungodly women just to spite his parents (Genesis 28:8). I wonder how Isaac felt about Rebekah's treachery and deceptions, not only against *his* favorite son, but against him too. Can you say "family dysfunction?"

Among the many great abuses against children is the emotional abuse associated with favoring one child over another. Each child is unique and *"fearfully and wonderfully made"* as part of the family. Even though my girls are identical twins, there is really nothing identical about them to me. They are precious individuals with distinct personalities, gifts, abilities, weaknesses and strengths. I've so enjoyed how different they are from each other and it has been a joy to be their mother. Moms, be sure to tell your children how special they are to you and to your family. Reaffirm their worth as a child of God and also as a unique person in your family.

The bottom line for us is this: don't play favorites with your children. It is costly to your family in ways that may pass down from generation to generation. And it will certainly harm relationships in the present.

## Discussion Questions

1. Share a time when you felt most loved by your own parents? (Or the ones who raised you, if you were raised by someone other than your parents) How did this make you feel? How has this impacted your own parenting?

2. Share something that was helpful or an insight you gained from each of the common parenting mistakes shared in this chapter?

   • From Eli and his sons?

   • From Abraham and Sarah's story?

   • From Isaac and Rebekah?

152

3.  Reflecting on the parenting issues in this chapter, what changes, if any, do you feel that you could apply to your life as a wife or as a mom?

4.  What can we learn about God as our Heavenly parent from these verses?   How should this encourage us to parent our own children?

    Acts 10:34-35

    Ephesians 2:4-7

    1 Peter 1:14-19

5. Discuss ways that you can avoid some of the common parenting mistakes discussed in this chapter. What are some practical steps you can put into action today?

6. Share one insight, thought or verse that was most meaningful to you from this chapter and why.

# Chapter 11
# Forever on My Knees

Grace and Space

For me this is the hardest chapter to put down into words because I am still learning it and living it. It's about prayer, it's about love, it's about letting go and giving our children grace and space to live as individuals. It's about really understanding that our children are precious gifts on loan to us from God. I got to have my two beautiful twin daughters under roof for 18 years and I can't remember any time they weren't just the joy of my life. (And of course, they still are.) Now, that isn't to say that I didn't get frustrated, angry, and weary, because I've already shared that I did. The hardest part of parenting for me was and will continue to be dealing with any pain that they suffer, from bloody knees to broken hearts. Today their struggles are adult struggles, but they are still my children (my husband will always refer to them as his "baby girls") and so I suffer right along with them, but mostly in prayer.

I began praying for and about my children long before they were born. Many of you who are reading this have done the same. I prayed for healthy development when I carried "my baby", for safe delivery, and for countless other things through babyhood, toddlerhood, elementary days, the teen years, college, and young adulthood. I have prayed from their childhood about their future mates and both the days that each walked down the aisle to marry their guys, I was astounded by the joy of seeing these prayers answered. Those were magical, miraculous moments for me.

I have not stopped praying and will probably forever be on my knees for my girls and their guys until the day that we all are in the presence of the Lord where there will be no more sickness, no more dying, no more war, no more worries about our children or anything else for that matter. I actually do long for that day.

I long for the day for many reasons. First, I'll get to meet my Savior face to face. To see Amazing Grace realized is hard to even comprehend. We'll dance on streets of gold, sing and laugh, and be reunited with those in Christ who have gone there ahead of us, waiting for us. There will be an understanding of things not understood now.

When the girls were about 15 months old, we got another surprise. I was pregnant again. This was indeed a surprise to both of us. Whoa! I was going to have three children aged two and under in just a few short months. We were surprised, but of course, God was not.

Richard and I decided since we'd had surprise twins, and this baby was a surprise, we should probably see a doctor more experienced in high-risk pregnancies to make sure there were no more surprises. But we were thinking about the kind of surprises that we had experienced before. Our first visit to the doctor, however, brought a surprise that we had never considered. A routine ultrasound showed that our new little one, our third baby girl, had a genetic problem. The doctor began to share about our options.

Dazed, I sat in the doctor's office not able to say anything. Trying to hear, trying to process. What was he even saying? I do remember this: Richard quickly stopped the doctor from laying out any options regarding abortion. It was not an option. It was no choice. This was our daughter. She was our baby. Our Shannon.

Shannon's Story

The weeks were difficult following that news. There was talk of treatment while Shannon was developing, but that would require a special test to understand what was happening. This was a test where they drew amniotic fluid from me for analysis to see what was going on with Shannon. The results were not so conclusive for treatments, but did confirm Shannon's genetic disorder. I was told that most babies with her type of disorder do not survive the first trimester. Shannon survived 26 weeks.

There are not really words to express the loss that we felt and still do to this day. It is much easier to talk about as the years have gone by, well, most of the time. It was interesting though because people really didn't talk much about it with me other than to ask me if I was feeling better, as though I had just recovered from the flu. Yet, it was just their way of dealing with my loss and offering me comfort, so I received it. Another opportunity to live in grace.

But why did we only get to have Shannon for this short period of time? I do not know, but I have been encouraged and comforted by these words from Isaiah 53:3b. It says of Jesus that He was a *man of sorrows and acquainted with grief*. Jesus knows about grief. He understands. When no one else can understand what you are going through, Jesus does. He understands rejection, He understands sorrow, He understands it all. So I have had to learn to take all my inability to understand, my sorrow for what I had lost, the daughter we would not get to see take first steps, say first words, laugh, cry, or grow up and place her into the arms of the One who was and is acquainted with sorrow and grief.

It was the first of many experiences with my children that I was going to have to learn about grace and space. Children are a gift from the Lord. But, I don't really own that gift. Our children were given to us to steward, to shepherd, to guide, to steer, to love and raise for God's purposes, but they are not ours to control or keep. Just to love. And so was Shannon. She was ours to love for the short stay within me. She came for God's purpose and plans that I'll understand better when we are all united together in the place He has prepared for us. But for the years since she came and went, there has been the opportunity to live in the grace and space between us.

Letting Go

Letting go has been the hardest part of mothering. Letting go of a daughter I didn't get to mother. Letting go of my two daughters I was privileged to raise and release from our nest to make their own. There continues to be a letting go of what *was* in order to enjoy what God has anew today. This too is part of the process of growing as a woman.

We spend a lifetime figuring out how to teach our kids this and point out that and correct this, guarding against this, protecting from that... and then we blink and they are grown and planning their own futures. It's a glorious thing, but not without its own sorrow and grief. It's a chapter in the book that ends, but it's not the end of the book. There is more God is writing, but it was a precious chapter of life that holds sweet treasure. Jesus understands this too. It's part of His process, not only for our children, but for us.

While we want our children to grow up and lead healthy and productive lives, it means that we have to let go. We must give them the grace to grow up and the space to do it. This too is good because grandchildren can't come if children don't grow and go. This is another book for a future time.

It's important to learn how to let go appropriately. As I shared earlier, too many parents let go too soon and we watched as their kids "crashed and burned." But we also saw parents who wouldn't let go and the consequences were equally bad. Some kids so desperate for freedom tore hard against the iron apron strings, damaging and destroying their relationships with each other. Sadly, some kids never left home because they were never given the freedom to try out their wings, fly, and leave the nest—equally devastating.

A Sacred Connection

But how do we find our new place in our children's lives when they are young adults? How do we find our footing again? In some ways it is really like starting all over. Yet is has been a wonderful time of just focusing on my husband and our ministries together. We've are enjoying this season of our lives very much. It's a wonderful time in life, but one where prayer continues to provide a sacred connection to my children. I think I see this more clearly than ever; nothing I can do for my children could be more significant than the prayers I offered and continue to offer to the Lord on their behalf. We prayed before their lives began and will continue as long as we have life in us.

Without prayer, teaching my kids all the right things to do or not to do would have had value, but would have lacked the Spirit-moving power in my heart to do it right and prepare their hearts to receive it. Without prayer, reproof would have become a power trip to put our kids in their place or to vent our own unresolved issues, instead of yielding to God's gentle guiding touch. Without prayer, correction could have corrupted into abuse, rather than giving the Spirit of God the opportunity to guide the type of correction needed to train my children's hearts in righteous and to keep my own heart in check with Him.

In prayer and in His Word, we can meet God. It is only through God's movement in our lives that we can accomplish anything. It is only through His Spirit that we have anything to offer or give to our children that is of lasting importance. Prayer is not just important, it is essential.   James 5:16b gives us this insight regarding prayer: *the prayers of the righteous accomplish much.*  God invites us to pray all the time, not to manipulate Him like a genie in the bottle, but to truly seek Him.  That alone accomplishes much.

Crazy Powerful

Prayer is still such a mystery to me.  Why would an all sovereign, all powerful Creator God invite you and me to share our inner most thoughts and worries and fears with Him?  Why does He invite us to *"ask and it shall be given to you, seek and you shall find, knock and it shall be opened to you"* (Matthew 7:7) when He already knows us, inside and out?  Why does He invite us to *"come all who are weary and burdened with heavy loads and I will give you rest?"* (Matthew 11:28)  Why is this important to Him?

That's too big of a theological question for me to fully understand, but I think I can grasp just a little bit of it having had children of my own.  I think, in part, it is because of His Father, Daddy heart.  Prayer is the opportunity to express our heart to the Lord, for sure, but more importantly it is God's opportunity to open our hearts and minds, revealing Himself and directing us in His will, His thoughts, and His heart.

God desires to fellowship with His children just as we desire that fellowship with our children.  Think about how much you want to be with your children, how you want them close to love and care for, to guard, guide, protect, and just enjoy. I don't think I'll understand this side of heaven the deep, deep love of Jesus.   It is just incomprehensible.   We are His children and He loves us.  Being a parent has given me just a little taste of what His love must be like as I think of how much I love my own children.  Love is crazy powerful, isn't it?  And God is love.

Safe from the Storm

When the girls were small we could guarantee that the first crack of thunder on a stormy night would be immediately followed by the pattering of little feet running down the hall toward our bedroom.  It was not the norm for the girls to sleep with us in our bedroom, but we always had the heart to welcome them in on these nights for comfort and reassurance that they were safe from storms and that all was well.

This is how prayer is in my life.  I run to my heavenly Father all throughout my day seeking His reassurance, His comfort, His guidance, His wisdom, His help, His peace, for so many things, and especially as it relates to my own children—still. I still need to know that we are safe with Him and that all is well.  And in His welcoming place, I've drawn the strength to press on when I've been so scared, so sick, so tired, so frustrated, so mad, so hurt, and so sad.  In this safe place, He is teaching me to let go and give the grace and space my adult children need.

This is the grace of God at work in my life. This is the grace that has helped me to continue to rise up and follow Him as He leads me in new roles and new purposes with my adult children.

My prayer is that you too will find yourself often running down the hall into the arms of your Lord and Savior for the strength, wisdom, courage, and hope that you need to rise up and be the mother and the wife that God has called you to be too. It's no small task to fulfill these roles as a woman, but there is nothing more significant that you will do in your lifetime. And He is right there cheering you on.

## About the Author

Lee Sumner is a Bible-based speaker, teacher, and mentor to women, having served in women's ministry for over 25 years, including a full-time ministry position in a large church in Southern California. Lee has written Bible studies for women on a variety of topics, including marriage and family issues.

Currently living in Arizona, Lee serves on the Board of Directors of a non-profit organization for women focused on marriage and family matters, where she also teaches and counsels women. Lee ministers to women in the Phoenix area through her public speaking, writing, as well as in her local church family.

Lee and her husband Richard have been married over thirty years, raised two beautiful daughters, now married to special young men. Lee also serves with her husband in leadership for marriage and family ministry in their local church.

Lee welcomes the opportunities to speak to women's groups as well as with her husband to couples for weekend retreats and seminars. If you would like to invite Lee Sumner to be a speaker at your next women's event or retreat, please contact her at OneHeartPublishing@gmail.com.

# The Most Important Question of Your Life

The most important question of your life and one that you must know the answer to is this one: Do you know Jesus Christ as your Lord and Savior? Knowing the answer to this question is an eternal imperative for each of us. The Lord desires us to understand what is necessary to be saved and then to have a full assurance that we do indeed belong to Him for all eternity. In 1 John 5:13 the Apostle John wrote, *"these things I have written to you who believe in the name of the Son of God, in order that you may know that you have eternal life."*

The Bible is clear in telling us that we cannot earn our salvation. We cannot become Christians by attending church or doing religious acts, though they may be good things to do. But in reality we are separated from God because we have a sin nature. Romans 3:23 tells us that *"all have sinned and fall short of the glory of God."* And in Romans 6:23 we are told that the *"wages (payment) for our sin is death, but the free gift of God is eternal life in Christ Jesus our Lord."* In 2 Corinthians 5:21 we understand that Jesus, *"who knew no sin became sin on our behalf, that we might become the righteousness of God in Him."*

Jesus is our payment for the sin that separates us from a Holy and Righteous God. His payment is made available to everyone, but not everyone automatically receives His gift of eternal life. Romans 10:9 states "*if you confess with your mouth Jesus as Lord and believe in your heart that God raised Him from the dead, (then) you shall be saved.*" This means that we must acknowledge that we are sinners and cannot offer any solution for our sin problem, but embrace the payment that Jesus offered in our place. To be saved, we must accept that Christ's death as the only payment for that sin. It is then that we can receive the righteousness of Christ and know that we have eternal life in Him. 1 John 5:12 says "*he who has the Son has the life; he who does not have the Son of God does not have the life.*"

So the question is this: Do you have the Son? Have you confessed that your sin has separated you from a Holy God? And will you repent (turn, go the other direction) from that sin and receive Christ's payment for that sin? Will you confess Jesus as your Lord and Savior? If you have never done this, will you do in right now and know that you have the assurance of your eternal destination?

If you have any questions regarding God's plan of salvation and eternal life for you, will you please contact us at OneHeartPublishing@gmail.com?

169

# *Notes and References*

*All Bible passages quoted are from the New American Standard Version of The Lockman Foundation (1977) unless otherwise indicated and are listed in order as referenced in each chapter.*

Introduction
Titus 2:3-5

## Chapter 1: The Best Job Ever
Psalm 139:14, John 10:10, Jeremiah 29:11

## Chapter 2: What Does He Know?
James 1:19, Ephesians 5:33, Proverb 1:7, Psalm 68:5, Ephesians 3:20, 1 Peter 3:1-2, Proverbs 12:18, Proverbs 16:21

## Chapter 3: Who's in Control?
1 Corinthians 11:3, John 4:7-26, Luke 8:2-3, Luke 10:38-42, 1 Peter 3:7, Matthew 8:14, Ecclesiastes 4:12b, 1 Corinthians 11:3

## Chapter 4: Parenting 101
Exodus 20:12, Proverbs 30:12, Hebrews 12:15, Proverbs 10:1b, Proverbs 22:15a, Proverbs 17:22

## Chapter 5: Parenting with Purpose
Psalm 127:3, 2 Timothy 3:16-17, Genesis 1:3, John 1:14, Deuteronomy 6:6-7, 1 John 1:9, 1 Samuel 2:12
Josh McDowell and Norm Geisler, Love is Always Right, Word Publishing 1996

## Chapter 6: The Battle for Morality
Galatians 6:9, Proverbs 29:18

## Chapter 7: Back to Basics
1 Corinthians 6:19-20, Ephesians 4:32, 2 Peter 2:23, 1 Corinthians 15:33

## Chapter 8: The Necessary Nine
2 Corinthians 6:14-15, Galatians 5:22, 1 Corinthians 13:4-8, Psalm 16:11, Romans 12:18, Titus 1:7, Hebrews 10:24, Proverbs 12:22, Titus 3:2, Psalm 25:3

## Chapter 9: The Discipline of Discipline
Proverbs 10:17, Proverbs 15:31, Proverbs 29:17, Proverbs 23:13-14, Proverbs 22:15, Romans 6:23, Jeremiahs 10:24, Hebrews 12:6, Proverbs 29:15, Proverbs 13:24, Ephesians 6:4

## Chapter 10: Things We Need to Know
1 Samuel 2:29, Proverbs 3:5-6, Titus 2:4, Genesis 16, Isaiah 55:8-9, Genesis 25:28, Genesis 28:8

## Chapter 11: Forever on My Knees
Isaiah 53:3b, James 5:16b, Matthew 7:7, Matthew 11:28

Notes

Notes

Notes

Made in the USA
Charleston, SC
20 September 2013